TO

THE SATURDAY BOOK

NINETEENTH YEAR

THE SATURDAY BOOK

EDITED BY JOHN HADFIELD

19

THE MACMILLAN COMPANY

THE SATURDAY BOOK

was founded in 1941 by Leonard Russell
and has been edited since 1952 by John
Hadfield. This nineteenth annual issue
was printed at Tiptree in Essex by
The Anchor Press, Ltd., and bound by
Taylor Garnett Evans & Co., Ltd., in
Watford, Herts

THE FRONTISPIECE reproduces an
early nineteenth-century Staffordshire
pottery group in the Fitzwilliam
Museum, Cambridge.

INTRODUCTION

WE WERE umpiring in the annual Authors *v*. Publishers cricket match in Vincent Square. 'And what,' said the bearded poet, as he prepared to bowl, 'is the theme of this year's *Saturday Book*?' We were searching for the answer when he appealed for lbw against the batsman, a former Test player. 'Out,' we replied vaguely, though the ball would manifestly have passed at least a dactye outside his leg-stump. 'It's marvellous how you think up fresh themes for the *Saturday Book* year after year,' said the bearded poet enthusiastically. 'It goes from strength to strength.'

We are reminded of this conversation as we study the colour proofs of the frontispiece and wonder exactly *why* we chose it as a frontispiece. There appears to be no good reason other than its gaiety, curiosity, and vigour. Or was there, perhaps, some free association between the potter's menagerie and Sir Winston's butterflies (page 33) or Kenneth Allsop's kestrel (page 45)?

Never mind. Frontispiece apart, it is evident that this year's *S.B.* has indeed got something which approximates to a theme. More than half the contents could be card-indexed in the bearded poet's mind as Recreation, Art of. 'The theme of this year's *Saturday Book*,' he will write (we hope, for he is a reviewer too), 'is one of peculiar relevance to the problem of leisure in the atomic age. . . .'

Of course, it's a swizz, really. We merely put in all the bits and pieces of this and that which happen to have taken our fancy during the past year. Recreation has been the overriding theme of all the *Saturday Books* since the first one wandered into a warring world in 1941. The justification of the book—if it needs one—is that it is utterly unconcerned with work, problems, issues, movements, and trends. It is solely concerned with enjoyment.

The objects of enjoyment are usually unrelated and unpredictable. These words are being written under an orange-tree on the slopes of Monte Circeo (where Ulysses encountered Circe) beside a calm blue Mediterranean Sea. To reach this point, from the editorial desk in Great Portland Street, we have made a miniature Grand Tour through Holland, Germany, Austria, and Italy. What impressions are clearest in our mind? The hellenistic influences on Renaissance art? The interplay of gothic and baroque in Western architecture? No. What we recall most clearly is an irrepressible Italian boy clambering over the steps of the tomb of St Francis at Assisi, the lovely modelling of a bowed head carved in wood by Jörg Syrlin in the choir-stalls of Ulm Cathedral, the gaiety of a group of Austrians whistling 'Colonel Bogey' to accordion accompaniment in the Goldener Adler at Innsbruck, a Swallow-tail butterfly settling upon Trajan's Column, or the vivid colouring of a peacock painted on a ceiling in the catacomb of St Calixtus.

And that reminds us that an Answer to Correspondents is long overdue. Yes, we still have the editorial peacock whose accession was recorded in our fourteenth issue. There have been enquiries after his health from the United States, Australia, South Africa, and Hong Kong. He lost his first wife some years ago (she was taken by a fox). But he has married again, has a chick in Worcestershire, and is still as ornamental, amiable, and otherwise purposeless as the *Saturday Book* itself.

J. H.

CONTENTS

ELEGANT RECREATIONS

THE SATURDAY BOOK STORIES

PROFILE

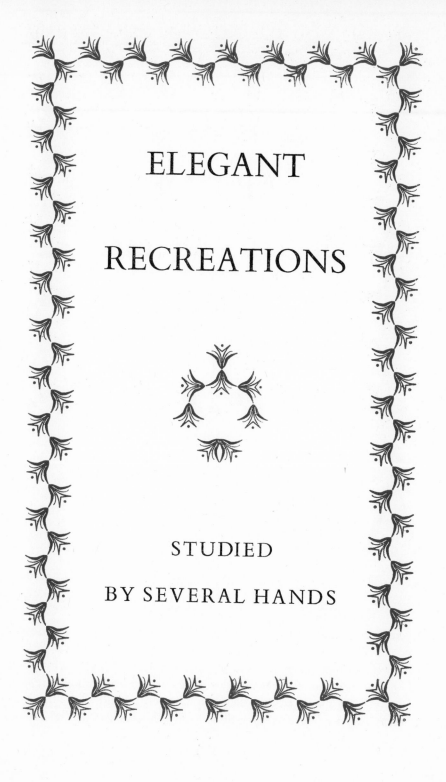

ELEGANT

RECREATIONS

STUDIED

BY SEVERAL HANDS

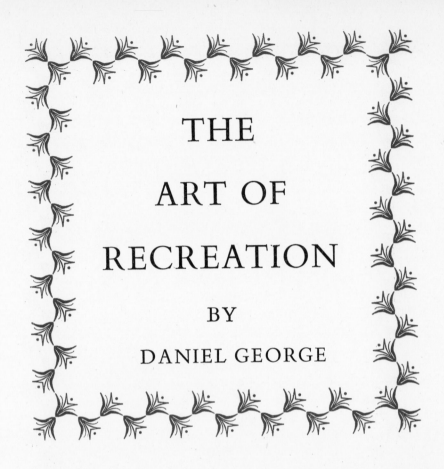

THE

ART OF

RECREATION

BY

DANIEL GEORGE

'ANYTHING but sport' was Bernard Shaw's reply to the en-
quiry, 'What are your recreations?' By sport he presumably
meant anything that involved physical exercise, though in
practice he made exception of walking and swimming. Here
he would have had the approval of Seneca who, according
to Isaac D'Israeli, saw something indecent in the spectacle of a man of
letters exulting in the strength of his arm or the breadth of his back.
D'Israeli was writing about the amusements of the learned. He tells us that
when Petavius was employed in his *Dogmata Theologica* 'the great
recreation of the learned father was, at the end of every second hour, to
twirl in his chair for five minutes'. Spinoza, it seems, would unbend his
mind by setting spiders to fight each other: 'He observed their combats
with so much interest that he was often seized with immoderate fits of
laughter.' Cardinal de Richelieu, on the other hand, did not disdain
violent exercise; he was once discovered with his servant 'trying who

could leap the highest'. And the logician Samuel Clarke diverted himself by jumping over tables and chairs. But on the whole the sedentary have preferred to remain sedentary.

Robert Burton, author of *The Anatomy of Melancholy*, could in the end find no relief from his own melancholy but in leaning over a bridge at Oxford and hearing the bargemen swear at one another. In his prescriptions for other sufferers, of course, he presents a formidable array of possibilities, but he appears to have had something against fishing; he quotes, with approval, Plutarch, who regarded it as 'a filthy, base, illiberal employment, having neither wit nor perspicacity in it, not worth the labour'. Izaac Walton was of a very different opinion, praising Dr Alexander Nowell, Dean of St Paul's, who spent a tenth part of his time in angling, and who, as Fuller records, left a bottle of ale in the grass, and found it, some days after, 'no bottle but a gun, such the sound of the opening thereof; and this is believed (casualty is the mother of more inventions than industry) the original of bottle ale in England'. Walton also commends the example of 'that undervaluer of money, the late provost of Eton, Sir Henry Wotton', who said of angling that it was 'a rest to his mind, a cheerer of his spirits, a diverter of sadness, a calmer of unquiet thoughts, a moderator of passions, a procurer of contentedness'. A later angler was the learned eighteenth-century Dr Thomas Birch, who camouflaged himself as an old tree. 'His arms,' says Thomas Taylor, 'he conceived would appear like branches, and the line like a long spray. In this sylvan attire he used to take root by the side of a favourite stream, and imagined that his motions might seem to the fish to be the effect of wind.'

Burton is cautious in recommending indoor pastimes. Of chess he says: 'It is a game too troublesome for some men's brains, too full of anxiety, all out as bad as study; besides, it is a testy, cholerick game, and very offensive to him that loseth the Mate. William the Conqueror, playing at chess with the Prince of France (Dauphiné was not annexed to that crown in those days), losing a mate, knocked the chessboard about his pate, which was a cause afterwards of much enmity betwixt them.' Naturally, Burton saw no harm in reading, though he did not expect women to devote much time to study: 'They have curious needleworks, cut-works, spinning, bone-lace, and many pretty devices of their own making.' Music he allows, both the making of it and the listening to it. He might have reminded us, but does not, of Nero's fiddling (it was

[11]

actually harping) and of his conscripted audience of nobles and senators who, all a long summer's day, would have to endure his harping and singing; 'and if any man happened, by long sitting, to sleep or by any other countenance to show himself to be weary, he was suddenly bobbed on the face by the servants of Nero for that purpose attending'.

Another musical emperor was Louis XI, who, being keen on new instruments, ordered the Abbot of Baigne to provide a concert of swines' voices. We are informed by Bayle (quoting from Bouchet's *Annales d'Aquitaine*) that the abbot mustered a great number of hogs, covered them with velvet, and constructed an organ the keys of which were provided 'with little spikes, which pricked the hogs' and 'made 'em cry in such time and consort as highly delighted the king and all his company'. To come nearer our own time, Montagu Williams tells us that the favourite hobby of Charles Peace, the notorious criminal, was the collecting of musical instruments, on which 'he never played anything but sacred music'. Before going out a-burgling he played the violin, while one of his housekeepers sang and the other accompanied him on the piano.

With music-making and singing Burton brackets dancing as conducing to mirth: 'Ctesias reports of a Persian king that had 150 maids attending at his table, to play, sing, and dance by turns; and Lil. Geraldus of an Egyptian Prince that kept nine virgins to wait upon him, and those of the most excellent feature and sweet voices, which afterwards gave occasion to the Greeks of that fiction of the nine Muses. The King of Ethiopia in Africa, most of our Asiatic Princes have done so and do; those Sophies, Mogors, Turks, &c. solace themselves after supper amongst their Queens and Concubines, taking great pleasure . . . to see and hear them sing and dance.' Although music is not included in it, a diversion of the Great Turk, as reported by Sir George Courthop, may be mentioned here. He describes a pond made of porphyry stone in the middle of a grove. The trees are hung with carpets 'that none can see into it, or dare approach near it'. Into this pond the Great Turk puts his concubines 'stark naked and shooteth at them with certain pellets that stick upon them without any damage to their bodies. And sometimes he lets the water in such abundance upon them (for he can let what water he will in) that being above their heights they all bob up and down for life; and when his pleasure is satisfied with the sport, he lets down the water, and calls the eunuchs who wait upon his women to fetch them out if alive.'

As for the royalty of Persia, Xerxes is praised for devoting his spare

time to the planting of innumerable fruit trees, and Sardanapalus detested for dressing as a woman and occupying himself with spinning. Transvestism was one of the diversions of Henri III of France. 'In 1577 he frequented public entertainments in female attire, his doublet open, his bosom bare, with a necklace of pearls, and three little capes as they were then worn by the ladies of the court.' Our own Viscount Cornbury, Governor of New York from 1701 to 1708, appeared at a public assembly dressed as a woman, and, when remonstrated with, argued that there was no impropriety in it, since he was representing Queen Anne. He is said to have always employed the most fashionable milliners, shoemakers, staymakers, etc.

Henri III would also amuse himself by walking the streets of Paris with a basket hanging from his neck. Out of it peeped the heads of half a dozen puppies. De Thou estimates that he spent annually £12,000 on little dogs alone. The Earl of Bridgewater is reported by a Paris newspaper in 1826 to have made himself similarly conspicuous: 'His carriage is frequently to be seen filled with dogs. He bestows great care on the feet of those dogs, and orders them boots, for which he pays as dearly as for his own.' A dozen of his favourite dogs sat at table with him, each with its appointed chair, a napkin round its neck, and with a servant to attend to its wants.

Care of cats, dogs, and other animals has supplied the only recreation for many famous people. Pope says that Saint-Evremond used always to be feeding the ducks or fowls that he kept in his chamber. Dean Ramsay tells us that Lord Gardenstone indulged the love of pigs and the love of snuff. He took a young pig as a pet. 'At first the animal shared his bed, but when, growing up to advanced swinehood, it became unfit for such companionship, he had it to sleep in his room, in which he made a comfortable couch for it of his own clothes. His snuff he kept not in a box but in a leathern waist-pocket made for the purpose. He took it in enormous quantities and used to say that if he had a dozen noses he would feed them all.'

The cats of the Rev. R. S. Hawker must have kept him busy. He was usually followed into church by nine or ten of them. 'One of them having caught, killed, and eaten a mouse on Sunday, was excommunicated, and from that day was not allowed again within the sanctuary.' In the middle of the eighteenth century a Mrs Gregg, who lived in Southampton Row, was remarkable for keeping eighty cats. 'The maids being frequently tired of their attendance on such a numerous household, she was reduced at last to take a black woman to attend upon and feed them.' Jeremy Bentham's devotion to his cats is notorious, but he had inanimate pets as well—his stick Dapple, and his tea-pot Dicky. He took no exercise outside his garden in Westminster. Nor could Cowper with his cats and hares have been much more active.

In the days of the Regency the fashionable pastime was driving coaches. Among the members of the Four-in-Hand Club, writes Captain Gronow, was a Mr Akers who 'was so determined to be looked upon as a regular coachman that he had his front teeth so filed that a division between them might enable him to expel his spittle in the true fashion of some of the most knowing stage-coach drivers'.

If we can believe De Quincey, the art of spitting was at that time cultivated: 'The professors in this faculty were the hackney-coachmen; the pupils were gentlemen, who paid a guinea each for three lessons; the chief problem in this system of hydraulics being to throw the salivating column in a parabolic curve from the centre of Parliament Street, when driving four-in-hand, to the foot pavements, right and left, so as to alarm the consciences of guilty peripatetics on either side. The ultimate problem, which closed the curriculum of study, was held to lie in spitting round a corner; when *that* was mastered, the pupil was entitled to his doctor's degree.'

Jack Spencer, a young relative of the Duchess of Marlborough, drove a hackney coach through the city. Brought before a magistrate because he was quite naked as he drove, he is said to have exclaimed, when expostulated with on the indecency of his appearance: 'Naked! Why, I was born so, sir,' with an affected simplicity such as a man might be supposed to exhibit when a natural deformity had been mentioned.

The pleasures of the table have formed the chief spare-time employment and recreation of many famous people. Twistleton Fiennes, Lord Saye and Seele, was the greatest epicure of his day (early nineteenth century). He liked an omelette entirely composed of golden pheasants' eggs, and would drink absinthe and curaçoa in copious quantities. Of Vitellius, Roman Emperor from January 2nd to December 22nd, A.D. 60, it is reported by Suetonius that at the Dedication of his Great Platter it was filled with 'an oglio consisting of the livers of thornbacks, the brains of pheasants and peacocks, the tongues of phenicopters, and the milky guts of mullets, for which the bowels of the ocean had been

ransacked from the Carpathian Sea to the Straights of Spain'. Elagabalus, Roman Emperor A.D. 218–222, was so fussy about his food that when he was on the sea coast he would eat nothing but fowl from the remotest mountains, and when farthest from the sea, nothing but sea fish. He was assassinated.

The pastimes of most other Roman Emperors must, as Gibbon said of the Empress Theodora's, be veiled in the obscurity of a learned language. But it can be revealed that Domitian, who seems to be remembered chiefly because his favourite sport was catching flies, was also quite an archer: 'Sometimes he would set a boy to hold his hand at a good distance, with his fingers spread wide open against a wall, at which he directed his aim with that exactness that the arrows passed all between the spaces of the fingers without doing any harm to the boy's hand.' Caligula's pleasure was to pretend he was a god—sometimes Neptune with a trident, sometimes Apollo with a harp. He would even appear as Venus with a crown of myrtles, or Diana with a dart and quiver.

It is not always easy to distinguish a hobby from a mania, but a desire to reform the human race might, in some aspects, develop into a recreation. Alexander Cruden, for example, must have found some amusement in walking about with a huge sponge for the purpose of obliterating all rude words from walls. And that eccentric publisher and bookseller, John Dunton, who determined to extirpate lewdness from London, probably got some kick out of his efforts to 'win the erring fair to the paths of virtue'. He admits that he was exposed to 'perilous adventures'. Similarly, Walking Stewart, a regenerating philosopher, who wanted to discover the Polarization of Truth, cannot have been as bored by his propaganding mission as his friends were. He asked them to wrap up his books to preserve them from moisture and bury them seven or eight feet deep, so that they would be discovered centuries hence. He once had the intention of having his name inscribed on a rock in the Atlantic, in the largest possible characters, so that passengers in ships would see it and be induced to examine his theories.

There have been macabre recreations. George Selwyn, Horace Walpole's friend, was not alone in deriving pleasure from the sight of hangings. Thomas Warton, the poet, when absent from Oxford, could usually be tracked to a town where a hanging was to occur. Like Selwyn, he was an amateur of this form of sport, leaving a hanging for sheep-stealing in Oxford to travel miles to see a man hanged for murder.

[15]

Eighteenth-century nobility had often more active means of amusement. Fox-hunting squires, of course, abounded. Thomas Assheton Smith of Tedworth, Hampshire, followed the hounds until he was eighty, having been at it since he was ten. Even the miser John Elwes permitted himself the expense of a kennel of foxhounds and a stable of hunters. There were pedestrian hunters too. A tailor of Cheltenham used to follow Lord Segrave's hounds. In Chambers' *Book of Days* we read: 'Such was his fleetness of foot and knowledge of the country, that, after following the hounds from kennel to cover he would continue his progress on foot after the fox had been started, and contrived almost always to make his appearance at the death.' Pedestrianism was usually the result of wagers. In July 1809 Captain Barclay won £3,000 for walking 1,000 miles in 1,000 successive hours. In 1773 an attorney's clerk won a hundred guineas for walking from London to York and back within six days. Simeon Ellerton, who died in 1709 at the advanced age of 104, needed no wagers to set him off. He lived at Craike in the county of Durham, and from there would often walk to London and other places on commissions from gentlemen of the neighbourhood. He lived in a neat stone cottage which he had built with his own hands, collecting the materials while on his various errands. He got so much into the habit of carrying a stone on his head that he could not walk without one.

Boxing and wrestling were also popular. Sir Thomas Parkyns, of Bunny Park, Nottinghamshire, is stated to have been equally at home in the wrestling ring and on the magisterial bench: 'It was said that he could throw an antagonist, combat a paradox, quote the classics, and lay down the law at quarter sessions, with any man in all England.' He had another interest: he formed and kept with great nicety a rare and probably unexampled collection of stone coffins. 'Sir Thomas Parkyns never knew a day's illness until his seventy-eight year, when death at last gave him the backfall, and he died universally beloved and lamented.' The famous Marquis of Granby was a patron of the pugilist Broughton, and while sitting to the painter Hayman was suddenly taken with the desire for a set-to. 'The gloves were handed down, and to work they went,' writes Henry Angelo, 'turning over all the arcana of the painter's studio, and shaking the whole house with their weight, when the noise became so violent that Mrs Hayman burst in, and, to her astonishment, saw her husband and his illustrious sitter knocking each other's heads off like two coal-heavers.'

Charles Paulet, Marquis of Winchester (1625–1699), called by Burnet 'the riddle of the age', was an all-round if inconsiderate sportsman. Sir John Reresby records a visit to him in August 1687: 'His custom was to dine at six or seven at night, and his meal lasted till seven or eight in the morning. Sometimes he drank; sometimes he heard music; sometimes discoursed; sometimes took tobacco, and sometimes ate; whilst the company did what they pleased. They might do the same, or rise, go or come, sit down or sleep. The meat and bottles continued all the night before them. In the morning he would hunt or hawk, if the weather was seasonable; if not he would dance, go to bed about eleven, and sleep till the evening.' Burnet writes: 'He had the spleen to an high degree, and affected extravagant behaviour; for many weeks he would not open his mouth till such hour of the day when he thought the air was pure. He changed the day into night, and often hunted by torchlight.'

Shelley, no athlete, delighted in making and sailing paper boats in the Serpentine or the round pond in Kensington Gardens. The story that having exhausted the supply of letters in his pocket he had recourse to a fifty-pound banknote is apocryphal. Peacock says he would sometimes, in the presence of boys, launch a paper boat freighted with half-pence, and run round with the boys to meet it and scramble the money among them. A more private amusement of Shelley's was the rolling up of pellets from a loaf carried under his arm and flicking them with his thumb at passers-by. Keats could enjoy a bear fight, a prize fight, or a fight in his own person with a butcher's boy. Cricket he was not fond of; at any rate, he records: 'Yesterday I got a black eye—the first time I took a cricket bat—Brown who is always one's friend in a disaster tied a leech over the eyelid, and there is no inflammation this morning. . . .' Hazlitt was much addicted to rackets. 'I have sometimes lain awake a whole night,' he writes, 'trying to serve out the last ball of an interesting game in a particular corner, which I had missed from a nervous feeling.'

Of the elegant and harmless diversions—collecting pictures, matchboxes, books, stamps, fishbones, china, eggs, etc.—much more could be said than can be found room for here, but John Tradescant deserves a mention for his collection of curiosities which formed the nucleus of the Ashmolean Museum at Oxford. A catalogue issued by him includes such items as: 'Easter eggs of the patriarchs of Jerusalem; two feathers of the phoenix' tail; claw of the bird Roc, who, as authors report, is able to truss an elephant; a natural dragon above two inches long; the Dodad, from the

isle of Mauritius, so big as not to be able to fly; half a hazel nut with seventy pieces of household stuff in it; a set of chessmen in a peppercorn; a trunion of Drake's ship; knife wherewith Hudson was killed in Hudson's Bay; Anne Bullen's night-vail; Edward the Confessor's gloves. . . .' These compare very favourably with the hoard of the Rev. Mr Hagmore of Calthorn in Leicestershire, who was found to have accumulated 30 gowns and cassocks, 68 dogs, 100 pairs of breeches, 100 pairs of boots, 400 pairs of shoes, 80 wigs, 80 wagons and carts, 80 ploughs, none used, 50 saddles, 30 wheelbarrows, 'and so many walking-sticks that a toy-man in Leicester Fields offered eight pounds for them'.

Kleptomania as a recreation has never been practised on a large scale, but some well-known people have been addicted to it. Perhaps the most forgivable of them was Lady Cork, of whom Fanny Kemble writes: 'Whenever she visited her friends in the country, her maid on her return home used to gather together whatever she did not recognize as belonging to her mistress, and her butler transmitted it back to the house where they had been staying.' For lack of something better, Lady Cork once carried off a pet hedgehog. 'After driving a few miles with this unpleasant spiked foot-warmer, she found means to dispose of it at a small town, where she stopped to change horses, to a baker, to whom she gave it in payment for a sponge cake. . . .'

One way and another it will be seen that recreation can take an infinite variety of forms. Let Burton have the last word on the subject: 'Go on then merrily to heaven. If the way be troublesome, and you in misery, in many grievances, on the other side you have many pleasant sports, objects, sweet smells, delightsome tastes, music, meats, herbs, flowers, &c. to recreate your senses.'

SATURDAY PAINTERS

THE THAMES FROM HAMMERSMITH BRIDGE
by the Rt Hon. Peter Thorneycroft, M.P.

BY OLIVE COOK

H.R.H. PRINCESS MARGARET
by H.R.H. the Duchess of Kent

SATURDAY PAINTERS are not to be confused with Sunday painters. An even greater gulf divides them than that which separates *The Saturday Book* from *Sunday at Home.* Just as there was no *Saturday Book* at the time when *Sunday at Home* lay on the parlour table beside the Family Bible, so nobody had ever heard of Saturday painters when the most famous of Sunday painters, the great Douanier Rousseau, sent his 'Snake Charmer' to the Salon d'automne. Saturday painters, like *The Saturday Book*, are peculiar to the present age.

The term Sunday painter was coined to describe just such a man as Henri Rousseau, an artist without training, who was otherwise occupied for the greater part of the week, and who painted in his spare time. Nowadays nearly all painters except Saturday painters are Sunday painters. It is one of the strange paradoxes of the century that while there has never been more apparent interest in painting, never such a bewildering variety of well-attended exhibitions and crowded lectures on art, the professional painter has no real place in society and has been driven to earn his bread by every possible means but painting. He has in fact become a Sunday painter and there are today only Sunday painters and Saturday painters.

Saturday painters also devote only their leisure hours to brush and canvas, but, unlike Sunday painters, most of them have attained celebrity in the professions in which they are engaged during the week. All the Saturday painters whose work appears in these pages excel in a sphere which is not painting, and express themselves most fully in the work which is the chief business of their lives. For all that he was only a part-time painter, Rousseau's whole personality was concentrated in his art; his post in the Customs office and the little stationer's shop he afterwards kept were only means to an end. Gauguin, who began as a Sunday painter, soon sacrificed his respectable career as a bank manager to his ruling passion. And a similar course was adopted by the man who was probably the first of all Sunday painters, the little-known sixteenth-century Swiss artist, Niklaus Manuel Deutsch. He was an able, though not a prominent, diplomat, and became governor of a canton, but his heart was not in the work, and he eventually preferred poverty and obscurity to painting only on Sundays. The same single-minded devotion to his art characterizes the one Sunday painter who is represented here among the Saturday painters, to point the distinction between him and them. Mr Thomas Britton, the painter of 'The Boxers', is by profession a house decorator, but by inclination a picture painter. A dismembered orange box provides him with five excellent painting surfaces, and having sized and primed them with all the perfection developed by his training, the artist retires from his irksome bread-winning task to spend long, undisturbed periods at Rowton House in pursuit of the dominant interest of his life.

But this is only the least of the divergencies between Saturday and Sunday painters. Mr Britton's picture stands out from all the others reproduced here by reason of its style. The curious intensity of this work derives from the artist's complete disregard of contemporary and bygone fashions and movements in painting, his exclusive preoccupation with his own world of fantasy. In this he shows himself to be the true descendant of the Douanier. Both, of course, see with an unsophisticated eye; but there are unlimited examples of Sunday painters who are fully alive to contemporary trends and steeped in knowledge of the past, and who yet achieve an original expression of their unique vision. There was no trace of *naïveté* about Niklaus Manuel Deutsch, a highly cultivated man of affairs; yet despite his keen interest in the most revolutionary and influential painter of his acquaintance, Dürer, his profound absorption in his own visual experiences enabled him to develop a style as personal as that of Gauguin, a compelling combination of naturalism and fantasy. With the notable exception of Mr Spike Milligan's spirited allusion to current fashions in painting, all the Saturday pictures shown here are executed in a more or less impressionist style; they are variations on the powerful impressionist manner of the greatest of Saturday painters, Sir Winston Churchill. Saturday pictures are indeed the work of people too deeply involved in some other all-important concern to develop an entirely original viewpoint or to see through the eyes of their most advanced contemporaries.

What is it then, we may well ask at this stage, which distinguishes these Saturday painters of our own age from the famous of other times who have now and then evinced a talent for drawing and painting—from such men as Victor Hugo or Goethe, for instance, who both liked occasionally to make topographical sketches, one in a romantic, the other in a prosaic, almost scientific, vein? What is it that differentiates the trifling of these two with pen and pencil from the canvases of Miss Clemence Dane, also a writer? In every case the drawn or painted image reveals something of the dynamic personality that emerges in full force in the written work, for, as Miss Dane remarks, writing and painting are but 'two forms of the same thing'. But whereas for both Hugo and Goethe drawing was so minor, so casual, an activity that it did not even become a hobby, the Saturday painter, when he is not busy being a politician, a writer, an actor, or a bishop, works as ardently and as regularly as the Sunday painter, and is often known to cover acres of canvas.

The Saturday painter's approach to his work, however, is poles apart from that of the Sunday painter. The little that has already been said is sufficient to indicate that the Sunday painter shares the serious attitude to his art of the great masters of the past, who have loved painting to the exclusion of all else. It is an attitude which results in struggle and anguish more often than joy. Many of the masters have described their sensations while standing at the easel, and their words tell of despair and unceasing effort. 'All painting consists of sacrifices,' announces Goya.

'Art is not a pleasure trip, it is a battle, a mill that grinds,' wails Millet; while a Chinese painter of 1310 complains of the 'thrall of bonds and sighs' to which his art subjects him and of the dark period of 'bitter thought over the theme' which always precedes creation; and Van Gogh, one of the most vocal of artists on the miseries of painting, writes to his brother thus: '*L'art est jaloux et exige tout notre temps et tout notre force. Et quand on les y consacre on passe pour une espece d'homme dépourvue de sens pratique et que sais-je encore. Cela donne parfois un goût amer. Enfin il s'agit de se sabrer à travers.*'

'Nude' by Bernard Miles

[23]

The most salient and refreshing characteristic of the Saturday painter, in striking contrast to this record of suffering, is his sheer pleasure in painting. To him it is a delightful and wholly enjoyable relaxation from the stern demands of his everyday life. This is the point of view put forward by the foremost Saturday painter, Sir Winston Churchill, in his stimulating book on painting as a hobby. And many of his followers show not only in their pictures but in their comments how heartily they endorse this attitude. Some of these illuminating comments have been preserved in the catalogues of exhibitions of Saturday paintings held from time to time at the Trafford Gallery—exhibitions which are significantly entitled 'Painting is a Pleasure'. The Rt Rev. C. K. N. Bardsley, Bishop of Coventry, writes: 'I paint because I enjoy it, it is a means of escape from the pressing problems of a busy life.' Lord John Hope, M.P., echoes these sentiments with, "Painting is the most delicious of all hobbies and the most complete of all forms of escape'; and Lady Olivier chimes in with, 'I started painting as a pastime after reading Sir Winston Churchill's book and found it a most relaxing and happy hobby.'

Painting, it seems, is not only creation, but a cure for the ills of our hurried, urban, and over-mechanized age. But there is nevertheless the possibility that in some cases Saturday painting may turn out to be more than a therapeutic exercise; it is not always easy to draw the dividing line between Saturday and Sunday painters. At any moment any one of the talented artists whose work enlivens these pages may well become a Sunday painter, and exchange his cries of pleasure for the moans and groans of genius in travail.

Reproduced opposite: 'The Yellow Door' by Vivien Leigh (by courtesy of Charles Harding, Esq.). 'The Gates of Kenwood' by Sir Ralph Richardson (by courtesy of the artist). *In the following pages, except where otherwise indicated, the paintings are reproduced by courtesy of the Trafford Gallery.*

Above: 'Eucalyptus Trees, California', by Clemence Dane
On the right, above: 'Fishing Village', by the Rt Rev. C. K. N. Bardsley,
Bishop of Coventry
On the right, below: 'Sea Island, Georgia', by H.E. the Hon. Winthrop Aldrich

'Boxers' by Thomas Britton (by courtesy of Mrs Peggy Richards)

Above: 'Jamaican Scene' by Noël Coward (by courtesy of the artist)

Below: 'When Did You Last See Your Father?' by Spike Milligan
(by courtesy of the artist)

Above, left: 'West Indian Woman', by the Hon. Michael Astor, Editor of *The Observer*. Above, right: Self Portrait by Douglas Fairbanks. On the left: 'Bomb Site', by Mary Morris (by courtesy of the artist).

On the right, above: 'All Saints and the New Bridge, Newcastle-on-Tyne', by the Hon. Nicholas Ridley. Below: 'Portrait of an Armchair', by Lady Mary Clive.

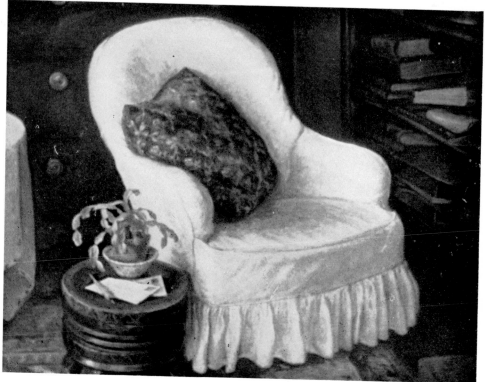

Swallow-tail Butterfly on Fennel. Photograph by W. J. C Murray

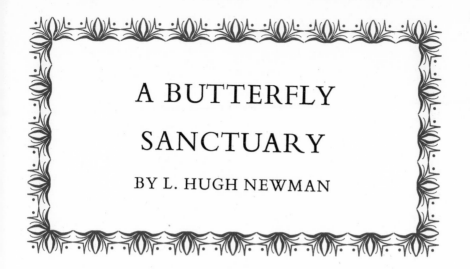

A BUTTERFLY
SANCTUARY

BY L. HUGH NEWMAN

A GARDEN can be put to many uses, and everyone has his own idea of what his 'precious plot' should contain. This does not apply only to the plants in the garden but to animal life as well. In days gone by the squire liked his strutting peacocks; today the fancier gives space to an elaborate pigeon loft or an aviary for his budgerigars. Some sacrifice a corner for their domestic fowls, ranking fresh eggs above cabbages and carrots. The eccentric may even dote on a donkey.

Fish and birds are the most popular garden animals, while insects, on the whole, are suspect and discouraged. Bees are, of course, the exception, and even if you don't admire the architecture of a modern hive there is something restful and reassuring about the hum of a bee-loud orchard in the spring. Butterflies are favoured too, with the exception of the Cabbage Whites; but unless you are an entomologist you may not realize that you can do a great deal to encourage these beautiful creatures to visit your garden, and perhaps to breed there as well.

Sir Winston Churchill, whose interests have always been wide and varied, noticed some years ago that there were not enough butterflies in his garden. Characteristically, he decided to do something about it. To begin with, he released large numbers of the most common butterflies, for the pleasure of seeing them fluttering amongst his flowers. Then he began to study the possibilities of introducing some of the rarer species.

The idea of importing the extinct Black-veined White, which had died out in Britain early in the century, appealed to Sir Winston very much. Under my guidance, 'nests' of the caterpillars were procured from

Europe and put out on hawthorn bushes in the grounds. We hoped that from this nucleus stock at Chartwell the butterflies would spread out into the surrounding countryside. Unfortunately, the experiment was not a success. An insect that has once become extinct has to fight against overwhelming odds to re-establish itself, and the Black-veined White always suffers heavy depredation by birds, as the chrysalids, which are attached to the twigs of the bushes by silken girdles, are very conspicuous. The few butterflies which survived the onslaught were not numerous enough to gain a foothold.

Sir Winston also tried to introduce Swallow-tails. A bed of fennel was made by the side of the lake to provide food for the caterpillars. This scheme, too, was a failure, but for a different reason. The farm bailiff had not been warned of the butterfly plans, and when he set out to scythe the grass and weeds round the lake he cut down the fennel too. So the butterflies could find no suitable plants on which to lay their eggs.

Apart from these disappointments, Sir Winston took tremendous pleasure in his butterflies. He was not in the least interested in dead cabinet specimens; it was the live insects he wanted. On his instructions I converted a small summer-house into an 'emerging cage', so that he could sit inside and watch the chrysalids hatch, and then, by opening a muslin-covered door, let the butterflies out into the garden himself when their wings had dried.

He was very concerned lest they should not find enough nourishment. He even went so far as to suggest fountains of honey and water in the rose garden. I was never quite sure whether this was meant to be taken seriously or not, but as he did not pursue the subject it was probably just a flight of fancy.

The study of live butterflies is far more interesting and rewarding than the mere amassing of a collection of pinned insects. Every butterfly has its individual characteristics and habits, and it is only by watching them alive in their natural surroundings that you can really get to know them well. You might pore for years over cabinet drawers until you knew every scale on their wings, but you would still be ignorant of their mode of flight, their courtship play, the way they lay their eggs, and the life-history of their caterpillars. It is only out of doors, in the sunshine, that you can see these things; and where better to begin than in your own garden?

Butterflies have excellent sight, and their big compound eyes can

even distinguish colours. They are entirely dependent on nectar for their nourishment, and by planting the right flowers you can go a long way towards making your garden the kind of place which butterflies like to visit. To you, a rose may be the most perfect flower in the world; but a butterfly will pass it by, for it has nothing to offer. The flowers that do attract them are always those which are especially rich in nectar. It is not difficult to provide a succession of these right through the summer.

In spring the clumps of aubretia, arabis, and yellow alyssum always attract the freshly awakened hibernators, and they also like to settle on the Siberian wallflowers. That low-growing, white-and-yellow annual, *Limnanthes Douglasii*, if sown in autumn, will provide a feast for the early butterflies. The old-fashioned sweet rocket is another great favourite. Valerian, a wild native which is well worth a place in your garden, and which will flourish exceedingly if your soil is chalky, is another good butterfly flower. Annual scabious, French and African marigolds, candy-tuft, heliotrope, annual chrysanthemum, ageratum and dwarf white alyssum, mignonette, tagetes, and Virginian stock are all easy flowers to grow from seed and will attract any butterflies within range. Sweet william is excellent, too, and, among the perennials, catmint.

Phlox and golden rod, pyrethrum, chrysanthemum maximum, and all the Michaelmas daisies will help to bring lovely insects to your garden, and if you have a large clump or an edging of pink sedum you may see half a dozen or more butterflies jostling each other on the flat pink blossoms. Butterflies learn from experience, and once they have found a haven of nectar-bearing flowers they will return to the place again and again. They love the scent of lavender flowers, and undoubtedly the best butterfly lure of all is the purple buddleia. This butterfly bush, as it is often called, was planted liberally at Chartwell when Sir Winston was creating his butterfly sanctuary. The rich honey fragrance carries far on the breeze. Butterflies are aware of it even before they can see the thick trusses of bloom. If you have a large bush in your garden you can be sure that any butterflies in the vicinity will certainly visit you.

Attracting butterflies is comparatively easy; but to make them stay and breed in your garden is another matter. It can be done, however, and the larger and more varied your garden is, the better are your chances of making it a butterfly sanctuary. With very few exceptions all butterflies need some particular plant for breeding and will not lay their eggs on anything else. The Cabbage Whites, as we know to our cost, favour

[35]

green vegetables and nasturtiums, but none of the other butterflies harm garden plants. Their larvae feed on a variety of weeds and wild flowers.

A whole group of our most colourful butterflies, the Vanessas, which include the Small Tortoiseshell, the Peacock, the Red Admiral, the Painted Lady, and the Comma, share a taste for stinging nettles. If you want these to breed within your boundaries you must be prepared to allow a patch of nettles to flourish in some sheltered sunny corner, preferably against the wall of a shed or outbuilding of some kind.

The Small Tortoiseshell and the Peacock hibernate through the cold winter months, and their favourite winter quarters are in dark outhouses where they hide among the beams. Soon after they wake up in the spring, and have had a few days of flight and feeding, their courtship begins. After mating, the females start to search for suitable nettle patches. They lay their huge egg batches on the undersides of the leaves, and when the spiny caterpillars hatch they feed gregariously in silken webs, stripping the leaves off the nettles in a very characteristic manner.

The Red Admiral, which is a migrant from southern Europe, lays its eggs singly, and the caterpillars join several leaves together with fine threads of silk and feed unobserved in these green 'tents'. The Painted Lady, another long-distance traveller, normally prefers thistles, but does occasionally lay on nettles as well. The Comma larvae may be found on nettles, hops, or wych elm.

If your garden is large enough to allow an open space to be left as a natural meadow, then you are almost certain to get some of the grass feeders to settle and breed. The Meadow Brown, a large, rather indolent butterfly, with a slow, flopping flight, bred for years on a piece of rough grass in my garden, and it was only when my sons became football enthusiasts and trampled the grass mercilessly underfoot that it disappeared. Small Coppers used to breed there too, their larvae feeding on the arrow-shaped leaves of the wild sorrel. In one corner I had a patch of bird's-foot trefoil, which for several seasons supported a small colony of Common Blues.

The Ringlet, the Small Meadow Brown, the Small Heath, and the Wall butterfly are four more which can be introduced to a grassy garden with a very good chance of success. They are all the 'stay-at-home' type of butterfly, which is content to flutter from flower to flower in a small area and has no urge to fly far afield. A small meadow with moon daisies and knapweed, yarrow, vetches, and perhaps a few thistles and some

[36]

Peacock Butterfly. From Benjamin Wilkes's *English Moths and Butterflies,* 1747–60

Above: Marbled White Butterfly. *Below:* Small Pearl-bordered Fritillaries.
Photographs by Gordon F. Woods

white clover, provides all they need. The grass should be left uncut until the end of the summer. If you cannot stand the untidy appearance, after that it can be cut with a scythe, but it should not be close-mown or the majority of the caterpillars will come to grief.

The Speckled Wood is another member of the Brown family with rather different habits. It is not an insect of the open spaces, but a butterfly of the glades. A small copse, not too thickly planted and with sunny patches between the trees, makes an ideal home for it. If you manage to introduce it successfully in a wooded garden you will be able to enjoy the sight of the cream-dappled butterflies all through the summer, because this insect has at least three broods during the season, from May to September, and even later in a warm autumn.

The Orange-tip is a delightful spring butterfly and when you watch it in a country lane it gives a superb demonstration of the disappearing trick. In flight the white males, with the brilliant orange tips to their wings, are very conspicuous and the black-and-white females, which look rather like small Cabbage butterflies, are also quite easy to follow with the eye. But the moment they settle you lose sight of them completely, and it takes very sharp eyes indeed to pierce their camouflage. The undersides of their wings are intricately mottled in white and grey-green, and when they sit without moving on the umbels of hedge parsley or the flower-clusters of Jack-by-the-hedge they look like an extension of the flowers and are virtually invisible.

The female Orange-tip lays her elongated eggs singly on the flower-stalks of Jack-by-the-hedge, lady's smock, and yellow mustard, and they are surprisingly easy to find. A good way of introducing these butterflies to your garden is to plant a fair-sized patch of Jack-by-the-hedge, collect some flower-heads, with eggs attached, in a near-by lane, and tie them with cotton on to your own plants. When the caterpillars hatch they will crawl from the withered stalks to the growing heads and begin to feed there on the developing seed-pods. Their boat-shaped chrysalids are attached to the plants and stay there all the winter. You should avoid cutting them down, and let the butterflies emerge naturally the following spring.

Primroses and wild violets are deliberately introduced into many a woodland garden, and the leaves of these plants are the food of several delightful butterflies. The small Duke of Burgundy Fritillary, which, incidentally, is not a true Fritillary at all, but the sole British representative

c*

of quite a different family, feeds on primroses. Strangely enough, the caterpillars prefer the old and decaying leaves to the fresh new ones, and so do very little real damage to the plants. The two early summer Fritillaries, the Pearl-bordered and the Small Pearl-bordered, feed on violets and, like the Duke of Burgundy, are usually found in rather open woodland or coppice, with plenty of sun between the trees and honey-bearing flowers like bugle and bluebells in the clearings.

The splendid large Fritillaries, such as the Silver-washed and the High Brown, are not insects that you could ever hope to keep within the confines of a garden, but if you are the owner of a stretch of woodland with plenty of violets growing beneath the trees and patches of bramble that will provide a feast of nectar when the butterflies are on the wing in July, it would be an interesting and worth-while experiment to try and introduce them.

The small Marsh Fritillary is a butterfly of a very different nature, slow to take wing and reluctant to fly any distance. The food of the caterpillars is the wild devil's-bit scabious. Despite its name, this butterfly is usually found on rather dry hillsides. The famous Hod Hill in Dorset is a favourite locality; but any suitable sunny slope or meadow which has plenty of scabious plants can become a nursery for these butterflies. Their larvae are gregarious, and in the spring the black crawling 'nests' are fairly easy to find when they first begin to stir at the beginning of April. I have recently moved house and my new garden contains a sloping paddock which looks ideal for Marsh Fritillaries. I have found that there is a lot of scabious growing in the grass. I shall try to introduce this butterfly at the first opportunity and I see no reason why it should not settle down.

The Skippers are another family that I hope to see in my garden before very long. These small butterflies, which 'buzz' from flower to flower rather like bees, love warm, sunny banks. I have a place in my garden now which seems ideal for at least three of them: the Small Skipper, which feeds on grasses, the Dingy Skipper, whose caterpillars eat bird's-foot trefoil, and the Grizzled Skipper, which lays its eggs on the leaves of wild strawberries. The steep slope in front of my house has all these plants and I will go out with a net and bring home a few dozen live females to release, hoping that they will not stray but will settle down in these new surroundings within my boundaries.

The Adonis Blue and the Chalkhill Blue are essentially butterflies of the windswept downs and will not thrive in a garden unless it is actually

Common Blue Butterfly (magnified). Photograph by Gordon F. Woods

Great Argus Butterfly and Passion Flower
From Benjamin Wilkes's *English Moths and Butterflies*, 1747–60

sited near their natural haunts. But apart from the Common Blue there is another member of the family which is very much a garden butterfly by nature. This is the Holly Blue, a charming little insect with two broods a year. Strangely enough, the two generations feed on different plants in the caterpillar stage. The spring larvae eat the flower-buds of holly and the late summer broods nibble the unopened blooms of ivy. Old gardens with holly hedges or well-established holly-trees and mellow walls hung with ivy are their favourite haunts. If your garden provides these two food-plants the chances are that you will see the delicate Dresden blue butterfly sipping nectar from your flowers.

The first butterfly to awake in the spring, even before the Small Tortoiseshell, is the yellow Brimstone. Here is an insect with 'wanderlust' in its blood. It will never take up residence in a garden, like the sedentary Browns and Skippers. You can encourage it to make a nursery on your land, however, by planting a few buckthorn bushes in your hedge. The passing females will stop, deposit a few eggs on the most prominent twigs, and then fly on, and as this happens over and over again your bushes may well nourish quite a number of the sleek green caterpillars and you may have a chance of seeing the fresh generation of butterflies when they emerge at the end of July.

Our finest native butterfly is undoubtedly the Swallow-tail, which is now confined to the Norfolk Broads. In days gone by it had a much wider distribution. With the efficient draining of the marshes, which took place over a century ago, the butterfly disappeared from most of its old haunts because its natural food plant, the marsh hog's fennel, would no longer thrive in the dry ground. Although in the wild our Swallow-tail always lays its eggs on this particular plant, the caterpillars will eat and thrive also on other things, including fennel, which is easily grown and very decorative. A well-established fennel plantation, preferably in an open, damp situation, would make a promising nursery for Swallow-tails, and in a good season young larvae put out on the fennel would have a fair chance of reaching maturity. The Continental Swallow-tail, which is much like our British native in looks, but much less particular over its larval food, would be even more likely to succeed. It is possible to obtain chrysalids in this country.

Some butterfly enthusiasts have tried out the idea of a butterfly cage in their garden, in much the same way as bird lovers build an aviary, but to be successful it must be really large. Many years ago a famous butterfly garden was made near Maidstone in Kent by an old friend of mine. A sunny walled enclosure was completely wired in with fine mesh netting and planted with honey-bearing flowers and the special plants and shrubs the butterflies needed. Protected as they were from birds, and unable to escape, and yet without that feeling of confinement which so often makes them batter themselves to pieces in a small cage, the butterflies lived their lives contentedly. Many of them, including the rare Camberwell Beauty and the southern European Cleopatra butterfly, actually bred successfully, and even hibernated in the attic of the house.

A cage, whether large or small, makes it easy to watch butterflies at close quarters; but keeping them confined in this way is not the same as seeing them at liberty in the garden. A cage is not a sanctuary in the true sense of the word. A butterfly sanctuary can only be achieved by trying to create conditions which will be so attractive to butterflies that they come of their own accord, and, having come, stay to breed.

Just as it is impossible to please everybody all the time, so you cannot hope ever to be able to make your garden a home for every kind of butterfly. Many of them are very local and need highly specialized conditions to thrive. Even to attempt to transplant them elsewhere is futile. But many of them are not so particular, and if you can provide food for both adults and larvae, and the sun and shelter they need, then you may well have the pleasure of seeing an increasing number of these graceful and lovely creatures in your garden each year.

I hope I have shown what a lot of pleasure you can get by introducing our native butterflies to your garden. But there is another aspect that I have not touched on, perhaps because it is not really very practical; I mean, experimenting with exotic butterflies. For some years now it has been my hobby to import the most outlandish species I can track down, breed them out, and then let them fly. I receive exciting little packets by airmail from India and Ceylon, where some of the finest and most beautiful Swallow-tails come from. Africa sends me mostly moths, but I have been able to breed in captivity, in one of my heated greenhouses, the famous African 'Orange-dog' Swallow-tail, and a lovely brown Fritillary. The most successful importation, I think, was the giant black-and-gold 'Bird-wing' butterfly from the Isle of Formosa. The female, when it emerged from its enormous chrysalis, measured just over eight inches in wing-span, and I should not be at all surprised if it reached the moon when I eventually let it go!

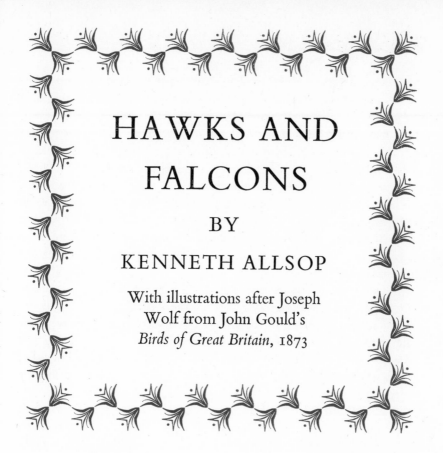

HAWKS AND FALCONS

BY

KENNETH ALLSOP

With illustrations after Joseph
Wolf from John Gould's
Birds of Great Britain, 1873

O NE MAY morning, when I was twelve years old, I
climbed a wall and walked quickly across parkland that
has now long been blotted out by the bricks of Outer
London. Then, a lightning-cracked oak stood in the
celandine meadows and I went straight to this tree. When
I was still a quarter of a mile away a sharp-winged bird left the tree and
began cutting wide arcs high in the sunlight. As I started up the oak, my
fingers and toes familiar with the stubs and crevices of its violated bark,
the bird swung nearer and cried out repeatedly with a shrill rapid note.

I did not wish to cause the hen kestrel pain, for I loved these little
slender falcons. But the mother bird's anxiety could not be avoided if
I was to carry out my plan, which had been awaiting fulfilment since
the first red egg was laid on the ledge above me. This was my most
intense desire, to become the master of a hawk.

I had last visited the eyrie ten days earlier, when the five young

ones were weak and tiny, crouched like soiled tufts of wool among flakes
of the rotten wood, blood-coloured fragments of their own eggs, and
bits of mouse-fur and bone. Now, I knew, they would be right for taking.

Hot from the climb, I reached up to the ledge and drew myself
level. The eyasses in their slummy litter scrambled back squawking
as their mother's cries rang out louder in the sky. I was in a precarious
position and wasted no time in selection. With my left hand I grabbed
the nearest eyass, thrust it down my pullover (tucked in my trousers
in readiness), and descended. As I hurried back across the parkland, over
the wall to where my bicycle was hidden in a ditch, and rode home, the
eyass was motionless in the darkness of my pullover; I could feel the
beating of its heart against my ribs.

In the safety of the garden shed I brought it out and placed it in the
packing-case cage I had prepared. It could not perch. Flopping off the
broom handle, it sprawled in the corner of the box, glaring at me with
its yellow-ringed eyes, the blue hooked beak gaping in fear. It was not
an attractive sight—Grock feet splayed out; wings, bare at the knuckles,
drooping like a wrecked umbrella; its body covered with a coarse grey
down and sprouts of brown feathers.

By late summer it had become beautiful—not yet with the full
bloomy vividness of an adult male, but rich in tawny autumn-leaf colours,
the tips of the flecked brown wings dipped in darker brown, the fawn
tail barred with chocolate, the breast cream and streaked in buff. His
brilliant eyes no longer stared with terror, for he had become at ease
with me. After those first few weeks I did not keep him imprisoned.
The shed remained his home. He roosted in the rafters, then later in the
elms at the foot of the garden. He came to my shoulder at my call when
I went with dead house-sparrows, shot with my Webley air-rifle.

I did not train him to kill and return to me by the ancient techniques
of falconry, because I then knew little of them, but I carried him about
upon my gloved wrist, and I still believe that this nervous wild bird,
perverse and tense with all other people, was calm with me because there
was a flow of feeling between boy and hawk.

My kestrel stayed with me until the following year, when he was
increasingly hunting for himself, wandering farther, and roosting in the
elms less and less frequently. Then one day he was gone from my life. I
did not feel sad about this because I thought happily of his freedom above
the fields, and when I saw a kestrel flying high across the parkland or

THE KITE

THE KESTREL

hovering, curved like a question-mark as it sought mice in the grass, I imagined with satisfaction that it might be mine.

I have never owned another hawk since then, for they are highly strung, delicate birds, requiring much time and attention, and falconry is a costly, complex art which can dominate all one's time; but that early passion which caused me to steal the kestrel has not diminished. I remain hawk-struck, a hawk fancier, an epicurean of hawks. All birds interest me and give me pleasure, but it is from the sight of hawks, and from my knowledge of their mode of life, that I obtain a particular sensual and aesthetic excitement.

Once or twice I have tried to dig back to the roots of this, and I suppose the infatuation found among individual ornithologists, who are often rather secretive about this exotic condition, is not really very complicated. For the admirer of wild creatures, Britain is a mild and moderate terrain, a huge suburban garden. Not a virgin acre remains. The swamps are drained, the forests felled. Amid the dairy farms, potato fields, hydro-electric schemes, nurseries, airfields, arterial roads, seaside promenades, tulip parks, and the subtopian tendrils that entwine between city and New Town, there is not much room left for rough moorland and lonely cliff ranges. Nor, in this tamed and supervised land, is there much room for bandits with hooked beaks. Gamekeepers' shotguns have sterilized entire regions of some specialized birds of prey.

In fact, it is now known fairly exactly how many birds of prey manage, in the face of mechanized cultivation and building, and the guns of farmers and keepers, to live in Britain. A field survey conducted by the magazine *British Birds* has put the strength of our seven rarer regular breeding species at the gloomily small figure of 1,200 pairs. Out of this, 750 pairs are peregrines, in itself a cheering number, as the RAF despatched extermination squads armed with rifles and poisoned meat during the war because peregrines were killing messenger pigeons; but now the old breeding stations, on coastal crags and inland mountains, seem to have been reoccupied. The remainder of that 1,200 includes: golden eagle—180 pairs; hobby (a beautiful miniature peregrine that summers in the southern counties)—60-90 pairs; Montagu's harrier—40-50 pairs; marsh harrier—10-15 pairs; and kite—8 pairs embattled in a few remote Welsh valleys.

In 1954 the buzzard population probably amounted to 30,000 birds, and it was spreading widely from the West Country; but the myxomatosis destruction of the rabbit, its staple food, may have severely set the buzzard back. There are no figures for the sparrow-hawk, which is generally distributed throughout wooded country, or for our commonest raptor, the little mole-and-insect-hunting kestrel, which without fuss adapts to the chopped-up marginal land of the Tube-train dormitories and even infiltrates the cities (in recent years London pairs have nested on Westminster Abbey, Greenwich Power Station, the Imperial Institute, and on various City buildings). Nor are there figures for the hen-harrier, a scarce lanky ground-beater confined to the wilder barrens of Scotland.

There is strong evidence that, given a break, these dwindled predators would make the effort to re-establish themselves in suitable country. Only the white-tailed sea-eagle, the last pair of which bred on Shetland in 1908, has completely abandoned Britain. The Montagu's harrier has advanced northward since the war. The marsh-harrier has slightly increased. The goshawk, even in early times an erratic resident, seems to favour the Forestry Commission's conifer plantations, and has bred several times in the past twenty years. The golden eagle may be slightly on the upgrade and has recently re-entered Ireland. The fish-catching osprey, wiped out by ghillies and egg-collectors fifty years ago, is again trying to nest on Speyside. Even the honey buzzard, always a rare summer visitor to the New Forest, has bred half a dozen times since the war.

Legislation now protects all British raptors except the sparrow-hawk, and there is a growing climate of enlightenment, a realization that hawks are not only worth preservation for their beauty, but because they are the natural and most efficient controllers of the legions of pigeons, rooks, starlings, and rabbits that plague our agriculture (and that goes for owls, the most efficient of rat-catchers). Yet, despite these causes for cautious optimism, the fact remains that the history of our raptors is a mournful one of savage persecution. They are now spread dangerously thin, many of them pushed to the brink of extinction.

The forces of destruction are still active: the pine-trees of Salisbury Plain are each summer freshly gashed by the climbing-irons of egg-collectors in pursuit of hobbies; the Royal Society for the Protection of Birds have to set up menacing defence networks in the zones of golden eagles' and kites' nests, as much against obsessional nature-photographers as against egg-thieves; the only clutch of osprey's eggs laid in Britain last spring was stolen by an oologist who got through the sentries under cover of darkness; and powerful game syndicates continue to flout the

THE ICELAND FALCON

THE HOBBY

law with their own rule of shoot-at-sight which, with a few intelligent exceptions, bars every kind of bird of prey from the air where pheasants or grouse fly.

One consequence is that Britain is rich in song-birds, the little passerines of our hedge-meshed countryside whose natural enemies are scarce. An additional consequence is that for bird-watching romantics the hawk has become the dash of drama, the flutter of a pirate's flag, the flavour of ancient nobility. There are the obvious visual attractions, for the raptors are all theatrically splendid—the falcon is as compact and keen of line as a combat plane; a soaring buzzard is as magnificent as a galleon in full sail—yet there is also the perhaps slightly improper allure that a chancer has for the solid citizen. Against a background of ordered society, the hawk belongs to the group of bold renegades with, say, the I.R.A. gunman, the desperado of Wild West mythology, the Outsider buccaneer of the Welfare State.

I know that this is a reprehensible and immature attitude. The serious modern ornithologist is the man who will with dedication spend five years investigating the behaviour-patterns of the house sparrow. It is excellent that such expert, intensive study is being made of the overlooked common birds. But, then, I am a shiftless and unserious ornithologist, and the episodes that have a fiery glow in my memory are those encounters with rare and daring hunters. . . . Memories of five Novembers ago on Fair Isle, when that remote chip of Atlantic rock was invaded by migrant Icelandic merlins, dark spiky birds which harried the flocks of snow-buntings under the stormy skies. . . . Of pulling in for petrol at a German filling-station and catching a glimpse of my only wild goshawk shooting across the road like a ballistic missile in pursuit of a turtle dove. . . . Of sprawling on dreamy summer evenings in Spreacombe Valley in North Devon while mewing buzzards rode the thermals above their pine-wood home, making my mind as airy and released. . . . Of seeing daily, just after the war, the pair of kestrels which were nesting in a bomb ruin north of Fleet Street and which, indifferent to the thunder and surge of traffic, hung on vibrant wings, watching for rodents above the rubbly patches cloudy with rosebay willow-herb. . . . Of inching forward in the dismal morning-traffic crawl along Chelsea Embankment and suddenly being jolted forward in the driving-seat by excitement at seeing a sparrow-hawk flash across my bonnet on the tail of a starling. . . . Of chasing a tiny jack merlin along an Exmoor lane in an Aston-Martin driven by Henry

D   [53]

Williamson—with the merlin gaining all the time, until it contemptuously swung up and away through a gateway.·.... Of spending hours at the foot of a lofty blade of rock on the Costa Brava waiting for the peregrine that was using it as a raiding-station to hurtle down with snicking wings upon a hoopoe or the swallows coursing the sea-marsh.

All these, and many other hawk-incidents (meeting many a sparrow-hawk, sinewy and oddly sinister in its sporty football-jersey stripes, blazing down a hedgerow in the hope of jumping a finch, or walking Norfolk marshes with distant harriers always in view, floating languidly above the reed-beds for the whole of shimmering hot days), are the plumes in a personal record of enjoyment of birds. Still, I am not alone in my fanaticism. For a small number of humans in every country, hawks have always possessed a strange glitter.

Falconry is the oldest of sports, certainly practised in China 2,000 years B.C. It was the activity of aristocrats in Persia, India, Arabia, and Japan centuries before it became the favourite outdoor pastime of our medieval nobility, who flew their muscular cream-breasted peregrines and spectacular white gerfalcons from Iceland at herons and rooks, leaving the larks and the small fry of the downland for their womenfolk's merlins.

In Western Europe falconry gathered about itself an elaborate ritual, vocabulary, and literature of its own, and a rigid table of etiquette and caste. In those equally class-conscious times, to carry a hawk stamped you as a gentleman more certainly than does a Brigade of Guards tie today. Birds exchanged hands at the equivalent to steeplechaser prizes—a nobleman in James I's reign paid one thousand guineas for two peregrines. The allocation of hawks was laid down in the fifteenth-century *Boke of St Albans*: 'Gerfalcon, a tercel of a gerfalcon are due to a king; Falcon gentle and a tercel gentle for a prince; Falcon of the rock, for a duke; Falcon Peregrine, for an earl: Bastard hawk, for a baron; sacre and sacrit, for a knight; Lanare and lanrell, for a squire; Merlin, for a lady; Hoby, for a young man; Goshawk, for a yeoman; Tercel, for a poor man; Spare hawk, for a priest; Muskyte, for an holiwater clerke; Kesterel, for a knave or servant.' So the raptors themselves were despotically divided into U and non-U—into the falcons (those with long wings and toothed beaks) or 'hawks of the lure', and the base hawks (the short-winged goshawks and sparrow-hawks) or 'hawks of the fist'.

Apart from the attraction of its ceremony—the birds in their

embossed hoods, silken tassels, and Lahore bells, the mounted falconers in ruffs, white stockings, and green caps, and the attendant entourage of cadgers (carriers of hawks) and austringers—it was a functional means of obtaining duck and hares and partridges for the table. The invention of the musket introduced more efficient and cheaper methods of killing, and falconry fell into decadence.

Yet it still retains its little hard core of supporters, such as the writer T. H. White, who described his goshawk as 'a Prussian officer in a pickel-haube, flashing a monocle, who sabred civilians when they crossed his path', and who stubbornly 'manned' it by the exhaustingly archaic method of sitting with it in solitude for three days and nights until its will was bent to his.

There is still today a British Falconry Club, whose members—perhaps stockbrokers, RAF pilots, business men—meticulously preserve that old procedure which is hard practical sense with a modicum of the mystical in it.

To get your bird nowadays is not easy, for peregrines' eyries are charted and protected, but a few of the more resilient romantics still prefer to take the risks (legal and physical) and slither on a rope down a precipice to a bone-strewn ledge to bring up their recruits in a basket. However, most that reach Britain are 'haggards', mature wild passage hawks trapped on the Dutch plains and traded like brilliant young centre-forwards.

The training is protracted and arduous for man and bird. First, the hawk's head is covered with a leather hood (to keep it docile in darkness), and jesses, or supple leather thongs, bell, swivel, and leash are attached to the legs. It is through the bird's hunger that it is schooled. Perched on the gauntleted wrist, it is fed with beef and hard-boiled eggs, meanwhile being stroked with a feather to soothe it and discourage it from 'bating', or threshing back in angry frustration and hanging head downward on its jesses. It lives in a darkened room of the hack-house, where it is carried about on the wrist between feeding, until, a few days later, it is taken out into daylight and placed to perch on a wooden block within sight and sound of humans and animals.

If the bird is settling and accepting its position on the wrist without sulking—for peregrines especially are neurotically finely balanced birds and easily made intractible by damaged pride—then begins the more difficult process of getting it to answer to the lure. The lure is usually a

stuffed pigeon or lump of meat tied to a length of twine. It is tossed upon the lawn and if the peregrine is keen it will instantly dash from its block to the lure, first a few feet distant, then many yards, to the extent of its leash. Next comes the vital moment when it is released and the lure is swung a hundred yards away. Will it answer? Or will it, spreading its powerful crescentic wings in full freedom for the first time, take to the skies?

Supposing that the hawk is good and responsive, the second crucial point comes quickly now—the release of a live pigeon within its sight. If the hawk kills and bears it to the ground, it will crouch over it until retrieved—but if it misses, it should, if the training has succeeded, circle and return to the wrist. It might not. It still has the opportunity to opt for free enterprise.

With that stage safely passed it is the time for experiment in the field, the release of the hawk in open country to 'wait on' at its stance high above the hills until a rook or lapwing flock comes by. Then arrives the sweet moment towards which all the months of patient endeavour have been directed: the 'stoop'—the thrumming nose-dive down the sky on clenched pinions—upon the singled-out bird, the strike, the pursuit, the ringing up to get above the quarry, another stoop . . . the relentless dog-fight, with the peregrine always mounting and swooping again. There might even be the rare delight, in the case of a particularly talented bird, of the deadly accurate collision on the first stoop, and the fluttering earthward of the shattered rook, neatly clouted with the hind talon as the peregrine has sheered past it with rattling wing-feathers.

It is for this reason that a handful of eccentrics labour in darkened rooms with stinking meat and bloody hands, and on cold spring days tramp the naked humps of the Bedfordshire and Wiltshire downs, obtaining their own rich and idiosyncratic pleasure from seeing their precious birds tip headlong through the air to assault and slay in the manner for which they have been so exquisitely designed.

Yet I myself think that the purer and completely anachronistic satisfaction belongs to the unidentifiable few non-participants who are content merely to catch sight of a kestrel riding a streaming hilltop wind or a peregrine skidding on lean wings, casually and unnoticed by others, around a headland noisy with gulls—those who surreptitiously share the independence and freedom of the wild hawk.

[56]

ON WINGS OF SONG

BY

J. W. LAMBERT

U P THE aseptic hanging staircases they pour, red tickets this side, green that, a turbulent flood defying the laws of gravity; and over them sounds the dulcet peal of the Festival Hall's warning signal—specially composed, surely, by Anton Webern? Inside the auditorium the long slope of seats fills, and in the boxes listeners wait like dolls propped up in a giant chest of drawers. Coats are folded, stoles adjusted, programmes opened. Soon every seat is filled; the house-lights go down a little, last-minute conversations take on, momentarily, a keener buzz, and by some psychic magnet all attention is focussed on the empty stage. Beneath the strange patterns of the organ-pipes, which seem to shape the perspectives of a dream-city, the grand piano waits, a darkly gleaming touchstone.

Then, up the half-dozen steps from the left, as applause swells fast from a side-drum tap to a long, deep kettle-drum roll, trots a very tall young man, frowning a little, head down, thick hair swept back. He moves across the front of the piano, and close behind him a shorter, stocky figure, his fresh face jutting between powerful shoulders, goes straight to the keyboard. Together they bow briefly, not to say curtly— they have better things to think about—to us, their courtiers; Gerald Moore sits, Dietrich Fischer-Dieskau stretches himself a little, looks

slowly up to the roof, down to the platform at his feet. By now we in the audience are quite still. Mr Moore sits with his right hand splayed out upon his thigh, and looks gravely up at his singer, who turns for a moment towards him, then gazes equally gravely back at us . . . and away the demi-semiquavers ripple:

> Das Wandern ist des Müllers Lust
> Das Wandern!
> Das Wandern ist des Müllers Lust
> Das Wandern!
> Das muss ein schlecter Müller sein
> Dem niemals fiel das Wandern ein. . . .

Puzzling that a little story in a strange tongue, set in a strange land, of a young man falling in love, being taken up, thrown over, and driven to thoughts of suicide should provide so unforgettable an experience. But Schubert's music speaks for all, and the human voice echoes for us the unchanging burdens of the heart.

It gives them wings of song . . . you flinch at the phrase? It has about it, you feel, a plushy sentimentality, a certain rapturous excess? What was good enough for Heine is good enough for me; indeed, I can think of no more fitting metaphor for this particular sensuous enchantment. Since the dawn of consciousness man has turned to it in moments of passion or glory or grief. Religion has required it, mass celebration demands it; and we in the West, individualists all, have shaped from it not only the ritual chants of communal emotion ('Abide With Me' at a Cup Final), but thousands upon thousands of highly personal works of art—some of them paradoxically artless, some gaily trivial, some universal as the sky—songs, in short.

Our complicated, specialized, and appallingly self-conscious age has a little lost touch with this particular magic. Some of us may sit entranced at the feet of a fine Lieder-singer; some of us may yelp with delight at today's microphone-bound hero of the Halls. But somehow the great mid-twentieth-century do-it-yourself movement has not yet extended to the world of song. Time was, I suppose, when the English were as ready with an air as the next man. Our folk-songs certainly have their own character, as strong if not as sweet as that of the Irish, Scots, or Welsh, the French or German or Bohemian (I say nothing about the hellish throat-racked keening of *flamenco*—well enough, I dare say, heard from a distance in the deep-etched Andalusian night).

We never were quite the nest of singing birds that some would have us believe in; in Elizabethan England not every barber's shop was a tumult of recorders at full hoot. Yet we must then have achieved something like the proficiency of Schubert's Vienna, in which boys and quite commonplace young ladies seem to have warbled at sight, and to general satisfaction, works which now make the stiffest challenge to the best professional singers. Even so, all too many references to music-making were tinged with a note heard down the centuries, and not easily distinguished from derision. In *As You Like It*, for example:

Jaques: More, I prithee, more. I can suck melancholy out of a song, as a weasel sucks eggs. More, I prithee, more.
Amiens: My voice is ragged: I know I cannot please you.
Jaques: I do not desire you to please me; I do desire you to sing. . . .

Jaques, here, is adopting another familiar English attitude: he clearly delights in singing, but is ashamed to admit it. This mysterious diffidence led to song becoming for some centuries the prerogative of well-brought-up young ladies and drunks; it was rescued, up to a point, by those natural enthusiasts the Victorians. But by that time it was perhaps too late; society was already undermined by the twin diseases of gentility and preference for the second-rate. A warning murmur from the collective unconscious forbids us to idealize the Victorian musical evening. Only the other day a music critic of *The Times* wrote of Mendelssohn's songs:

. . . The best of them, however, have a certain faded charm suggesting the drawing-room of Victorian times.

'A certain faded charm'—that is the best we can find to say for those overcrowded, overheated, overfurnished evenings; yet I am willing to bet that there was a good deal more to them than that—as there is certainly a good deal more to Mendelssohn's best songs.

Family and friends must have endured many a tortured hour; I can recall a few myself from much more recent experience—interminable stretches during which undisciplined bows hobbled lugubriously over ill-tuned cello-strings, pianos on which all the notes seemed to stick together in discordant pairs were remorselessly pounded, and gentle serenades sung as though they were recruiting ballads. Not that the amateur performer usually errs on the side of insensitivity; quite the reverse. Once I listened to a charming middle-aged woman singing a piece doubtless learned in her youth, and loved. The shade of John McCormack, I hoped, was watching benevolently over her as she launched out into 'I Hear You Calling Me'. As it turned out, if he was watching over her at all, he did so mischievously; for as, in her pretty, silvery voice, she approached the last repetition of the title-phrase, she clearly longed to put into the high sustained note to which it rises on 'call' all the yearning and love and regret she knew, so that a ghost of passion should breathe softly through. What with one thing and another she failed, poor woman, to produce any sound at all; most embarrassing.

And then there was Whitlow. He was short and square, and long before the days of the crew-cut his hair was alarmingly cropped; equally alarming was his manner, which even in what for others was casual conversation maintained a dreadful intensity, along with stupefying halitosis. He was a tenor, he told me in tones quivering with anguish, as though he longed to be a bass. Later, he stood by the piano looking out with naked eyes from behind thick glasses. Suddenly he raised himself on tiptoe and bared his teeth; and somehow kept them bared throughout his songs, while his head quivered like one of those jack-in-the-box dummies on a spring. When he came to Reynaldo Hahn's setting of Verlaine's 'Prison' St Vitus took charge. Flickering as though he were being seen on a very old film, '*Qu'as-tu fait,*' he fairly snarled, '*toi que voilà, pleurant sans cesse?*' And drawing a visibly enormous breath, '*Qu'as-tu fait,*' he repeated, '*toi que voilà, de ta jeunesse?*' His voice, fighting fearful odds, emerged as an alternation of a very restrained roar with a very coarse whisper. Heaven knows what agonies of self-reproach he was offloading. Certainly he had grasped the spirit of Verlaine; but what he was offering us was life, not art—not an aesthetic experience but a naked soul: again, most embarrassing.

There, of course, lies the trouble: embarrassment—the affliction which the English most dread and to which they are most prone. If the thought of himself singing quite paralyses an Englishman, the thought of somebody else doing so makes him equally uneasy. And just as in conversation he is almost certain to say what he least wishes to mention, so he is often impelled to drag up whatever he would prefer to leave in decent obscurity. . . .

Into the drawing-room files the little party. Dinner has gone well.

Conversation bubbles on, geniality reigns. Then one of the guests notices some music left (quite by chance, of course) on a corner of the piano.

'Now, my dear fellow,' he cries expansively to his host, interrupting his wife, who is talking about Mr Rattigan's new play. 'Come along, give us a song, eh?'

'No, no, really,' replies host, smirking. Guest, having regretted his request even as he made it, would like to leave it at that, but somehow it can't be done.

'Oh, please do, I mean it, we'd love to hear you—wouldn't we, darling?'

'Er, yes,' says his wife, who had been about to embark upon a description of the clothes worn by Mr Rattigan's heroine. 'Such a pity the old musical evenings have died out. It'll be quite like old times.'

'Oh, but I couldn't, such a bore for you, and besides, I've eaten too much, and smoked too much, and talked too much—hope I haven't drunk too much, ha-ha!'

. . . And so on for several minutes, during which host has gradually edged himself forward in his chair, stubbed out his cigarette, and finished his drink.

'Well, just one or two. But you mustn't expect too much, you know. I don't get much time to practise; for goodness' sake go on talking.'

Looking as little resigned as possible, his wife has moved over to the piano. She knows that she will be reproved after the guests have gone—if she backs up the suggestion that he should sing she has embarrassed her husband, if she does not she obviously believes in her heart that he's no good.

'What shall it be?' says the singer, removing from a shelf a mountain of songs, and beginning to pick his way through them. 'Schubert . . . h'm, h'm . . . Schumann, h'm . . . Wolf . . . not much room to breathe with all this food inside me, I'm distended enough as it is . . . Handel . . . h'm, h'm. . . .'

He thus continues, muttering to himself, for another four or five minutes. In spite of his suggestion the guests are afraid to start talking in case they seem to have lost interest. A numbing silence grips the room. At length one visitor, terrified into action, a rabbit breaking for cover, blurts out, 'I'm very fond of "Si mes vers avaient des ailes".'

'Don't know it,' replies the singer curtly; and then, realizing even in his abstraction that he has been less than civil—and besides, she who

spoke was the prettiest woman in the room—adds: 'Trouble is, I always think of worms instead of verses, and that spoils the mood, haw, haw!'

On he goes, riffling through the pile. This time his own wife's nerve breaks. To fill the gap she starts adumbrating a Chopin nocturne . . . but after a few bars her pleasant playing fades, for she has received from her husband a savage glare. Still, her desperate gesture has brought him back to reality. He comes up with a sheaf of songs as though he were an aqualung enthusiast laden with the treasures of the deep.

'Two or three things of different kinds,' he says, 'to give a bit of variety.'

Platform panic appears to be setting in, even in his own drawing-room; instead of addressing his patient guests he is speaking in a vacuum, his eyes unfocussed but looking, if anywhere, straight into the fire.

'First, one of the old Italian songs. Trouble is, people always sing these as though they were carved out of marble. There's a lot of feeling in them, really; one doesn't have to be cold to be classical.'

His wife plays the brief introduction to Alessandro Scarlatti's 'Sento nel Core'. He misses his first entry, which presents no complications of any kind. He scowls horribly, snarls 'Sorry, sorry, *sorry*' at his guests, and at his wife (in all other contexts he's a most equable and loving husband): 'Come on, let's start again, for goodness' sake.'

After that all goes relatively well. He proves to have an elegant light baritone. True, 'Sento nel Core' still sounds as though it were carved out of marble, and the long phrases of Handel's 'O Sleep, why dost thou leave me?' prove, though not disastrously, that his misgivings about singing so soon after dinner were justified. But his guests find it all rather pleasant. 'Charming,' they say, and 'That was very pleasant.' The tributes are welcome, though hardly specific enough in their praise.

Half an hour later, after five numbers from Schumann's *'Dichterliebe'* ('Well, I'll just do this next one, it's quite enchanting')—including 'Ich grolle nicht' with a gallant but far from effortless top A—Schubert's 'Du bist die Ruh' and 'Frühlingsglaube' ('You don't often hear this one, I can't think why not, it's perfectly delightful'), Wolf's 'Gesang Weylas' and 'Fussreise', and ('Just to give you a sort of English equivalent') Vaughan Williams' 'The Open Road' ('And I'll just run through "Bright is the Ring of Words" and "The Roadside Fire" ')—after all this the docile guests are in despair. Though he is no stentor, their host more than fills the small room.

A tentative hint: 'Must be pretty tiring, isn't it?' . . . 'Well, in a way, of course. But singing has its own exhilaration, you know.'

Perhaps some shadow of his guests' distress clouds his simple joy. There they sit, rocking slightly, heads throbbing, ears aching, stripped of all appropriate comment. His wife slumps on the piano-stool; she has an agonizing pain at the top of her spine, the result of so much anxious sight-reading. The fire is low, the glasses are empty, forgotten by the only man who can with decency refill them.

'Tell you what,' he booms with all his resonances switched on. 'Just to finish up with, a real contrast in style. I only do opera for fun, so you mustn't take it too seriously. First I'll do "Non piu andrai" from *The Marriage of Figaro*. Astonishing how many baritones spoil this, you know, by banging it too hard.'

Briskly he dispatches the mock-march—but caught up in the bouncing gaiety of the refrain duly bangs it too hard. Numb and helpless, the fireside group waits and wonders.

'And just to end with a bang, not a whimper, ha-ha, let's let everything go with the prologue to *Pagliacci*.'

He never really recovers from overblowing a simple E natural on the first page. Undaunted, he fills his lungs, pushes his voice out of shape and out of tune, wrings his hands under physical rather than emotional stress as though he were Lady Macbeth, and reduces at least two of his guests to the verge of fainting—one from pain, the other from suppressed laughter. . . .

Alas, I too have drifted towards derision; yet this is far from my intention, for I believe it to be true that

There is not any Musicke of Instruments whatsoever, comparable to that which is made of the voyces of Men, where the voyces are good, and the same well sorted and ordered.

So William Byrd in 1588; and certainly I have seen men, women, and children held and shaken by the human voice as by no instrument whatsoever, at every possible level of sophistication.

I have woken as a child in a starlit fishing town and heard a high soft tenor, almost an alto—and drunk, for all I know—breathe through the shadowed street, 'Queen of angels, Queen of angels, watch o'er thy servants on the deep'. As a child, I heard my father, standing by the piano

as my mother played, singing some drawing-room ballad or other—
'Give me your hand, that I may press it gently, And if the others see,
What matter they?' I have heard—not, I must admit, without astonish-
men—a naval engineer officer, at a ship's concert in Scapa Flow during
the war, hold spellbound 1,200 officers and men by singing 'Christopher
Robin is saying his Prayers'. I have seen a rowdy wardroom, flushed with
whisky and relief at returning to harbour, fall quiet as a single preoccupied
voice crooned to itself in a corner the 'Eriskay Love Lilt'. I have seen a
child of five sobbing through a suddenly mature mask of suffering as it
listened to Schumann sung in a language it did not know.

Deep springs are released in us by the human voice, controlled by
art and shaped by genius—or welling up in simplicity. Betwixt and
between, polite and guarded, we have lost the knack. 'You *sing*?' people
say to some apparently normal colleague incautious enough to admit his
little weakness. 'You *sing*?' people say to me (I may as well own up)—
and they look away with a sort of incredulous embarrassment (that strain
again!). I could understand this if the very idea of singing were alien to
them, if they were all tone deaf; but they will be as quick as I shall to snap
up tickets for a promising recital; and when they get there their pleasure
will be as great as mine. I shall see them, still as statues, breathless,
entranced. . . .

Gently the brook's lullaby dies away over the final heartbreak. Jovial
miller and flashy huntsman and faithless girl are all dissolved into a
point of rest; singer, pianist, and audience are one. Then a long sigh
sweeps down the terraces, the applause rockets up. The two men on the
platform shrink to their normal size, bow and smile and clasp hands; the
audience swells in contrast, from an almost invisible knot of concentra-
tion into a great mass of chattering, beaming, exhausted men and women.
Hazy and delighted, we stumble out . . . what artistry, what natural
gifts—and what a marvellous sequence of songs!

All the same, next time you ask a baritone to dinner, don't let him
loose on 'Die Schöne Müllerin'. Once he has been coaxed into starting—
and, remember, the cycle has twenty songs in it—he will certainly never
stop.

FOLLIES

BY OLIVE COOK AND EDWIN SMITH

W HAT is it that immediately stamps Sir Thomas Tresham's Triangular Lodge at Rushton as folly architecture and distinguishes it from a very similar building, also of the late sixteenth century, the Gate of Honour, Caius College, Cambridge, which certainly is not a folly? Both to us are architectural toys and both are excellent specimens of symbolism, the Elizabethan's favourite pursuit.

The Gate of Honour is an allegory in stone of the last of the successive stages along the academic path and makes sophisticated play with the Orders in a scholarly manner. Sir Thomas Tresham was a Roman Catholic whose ardour was fanned by frequent terms of imprisonment and large fines for recusancy, and the Triangular Lodge is a monument to his fanatical preoccupation with the religious significance of the number Three, the Trinity, the triune clover-leaf. It has three walls, three triangular gables along each wall, trefoil windows divided into patterns of three and multiples of three, and the whole is surmounted by a pinnacle triangular in section. Inside there are three-sided and six-sided rooms on three storeys and sunlight streaming through the openings flecks walls and floors with triangular shapes. This is the logic of madness. Whereas the gentle symbolism of the Gate of Honour is neither insistent nor peculiar to Dr Caius, and is expressed in a highly fashionable idiom, the Lodge is the embodiment of an obsession as idiosyncratic as the style in which it is built. One appeals to the intellect and is eminently suited to its purpose, the other is the fruit of forces stronger than reason and scorns utility. No lodge-keeper can ever have sent up the smoke of a home fire from the Triangle.

Unreason, present in a sufficient degree to provoke the prudent and

the prosaic, is the essential characteristic of the folly. The irrational element can assume a variety of forms, and knows neither style nor period; it can transfigure a country house, a railway station, or a hen-coop without entirely depriving them of utility; it can inspire sham ruins, castles, towers, and grottoes whose only function is to adorn a picturesque landscape; or it can lead a man to fling caution to the winds and embark upon some extravagant project which ruins him and, itself unfinished, becomes a ruin and a monument to its builder's folly.

Of the buildings whose purpose is so masked that we at once acclaim them as follies, one of the most obvious examples is St Pancras Station. Another instance, a border-line case, is Blenheim. Pope's celebrated objection to it confirms the strong inclination to classify it as a folly. It was nothing so mundane as mere lack of comfort which moved Pope to irritated criticism, but the fact that the house was not immediately recognizable as a building dedicated to dining and sleeping; Vanbrugh had sacrificed reason to colossal scale and decorative splendour. About Arno's Castle, Bristol, there can be no hesitation. It looks exactly like a toy fort and is built of iridescent blackish-blue blocks of slag with crenellations and Gothic ornament in startling white. No one would guess that it began life in 1765 as Mr William Reeve's stables, and that it is now a canteen and club for tramwaymen. An even more remarkable disguise is to be found at Rendlesham in Suffolk, where a cottage, by no means devoid of comfort, masquerades as a pinnacled and buttressed chapter-house. Not far away, at Tattingstone, a square-towered church of flint and brick turns out to have only three sides and no roof, and to have been built in 1760 as a screen for three cottages to improve the view from Squire White's residence. But all these are surpassed by the crazy fantasy of George Durant of Tong, who built a pyramid twenty feet high, known as the Egyptian Aviary, dedicated AB OVO, and intended as a hen-house.

The follies so far mentioned range in date from the sixteenth to the nineteenth centuries, and Mr Clough Williams-Ellis's activities at Portmeirion, where a mock ruin rises from rocks on the edge of the estuary and two-dimensional statues look just as if they had been carved in the round, show that even our own age does not lack folly artists. But the great period for folly architecture was the eighteenth century. Most of the sham ruins and spectacular prospect towers which are to be found all over England, giving compositional interest to a landscape or adding the right touch of romantic melancholy to a garden, owe their existence

to the eighteenth-century taste for the picturesque. Such was the pre-occupation with pictorial effect at that time that a sportsman like Mad Jack Fuller could quarrel hotly about the view from his dining-room and hurriedly build an utterly useless cone like a church steeple so that the scene should compose as he had sworn it did. A sober ex-Governor of Madras, Sir Robert Palk, wishing to commemorate a dear friend, Major-General Stringer Lawrence, quite naturally raised a folly tower to him in a spot that concentrated the wild, remote landscape and caught the eye of the distant traveller. He was not in the least deterred by the fact that Haldon Belvedere was almost inaccessible in its moorland solitude, that the elegant interior with its floor of rare marble radiating from the white statue of Stringer Lawrence would scarcely ever be seen, and that no one would ever dance in the ballroom above, with its Gothic plaster-work and its polished Indian mahogany. He could hardly have foreseen that the Belvedere would become a café and that hikers would sip tea at tables round the statue of the gentleman dressed as a Roman senator.

The garden pavilions and temples, with which our island is so thickly strewn, are also offspring of the same picture-making impulse, but only a few of these are true follies. Structures such as the Temple of Eolus at Kew and Burlington's domed Ionic temple at Chiswick are too completely in harmony with the Palladian principles of the day, too rational indeed to be classed as follies. The garden pavilion of Peckover House, Wisbech, on the other hand, is a true folly. Its outline suggests the Orient, and inside there is a stone seat and a grotesquely rusticated pedestal table in stone, with a gigantic stone melon fastened to its top. Palm-trees in the garden outside, their stiff foliage clinking like metal in the icy winds of the Fens, make a mad attempt to substantiate this dream of the East.

Ruins which were always ruins, surely the supreme expression of unreason in architecture, are nearly always in the Gothic manner, though occasionally the classical style is favoured. The castle at Wimpole is typical. It was built for Lord Chancellor Hardwicke by Sanderson Miller, famous for his work at Hagley and for the design of Ralph Allen's sham castle at Prior Park. There were more than two hundred feet of wall two feet thick and three towers each twenty feet across. It was well placed on rising ground, with a screen of trees behind so that no attention need be given to the back of the building. The towers were always suitably ruinous and the walls jagged, but now only one tower is more than a stump, the walls have nearly all crumbled into the nettles

[67]

hat thickly besiege them and the ruin, invaded by elder and hawthorn, must be even more convincing now than when it first graced the view from the hall.

The classical ruins at Virginia Water include the remains of work of true antiquity, columns brought to England 'by a wealthy traveller' from the Temple of Leptis Magna in Tripoli.

The extravaganza, abandoned uncompleted because its scale exceeded its builder's purse, is generally nearer in date to our own time than the follies of the picturesque period. One of the most spectacular of these is the ruined rotunda known as McCaig's Folly which dominates the town of Oban like another Colosseum. It was begun by John Stuart McCaig, 'Art Critic and Philosophical Essayist and Banker', who intended it to be a view tower, a museum and art gallery, a gift to the people of Oban, and a monument to himself. Jezreel's Temple at Gillingham is another and more celebrated folly of this kind. James Jershom Jezreel (*né* White) wrote a sensational book of sermons, *The Flying Roll*, while in the Indian Army, and these became the gospel for the sect he founded in 1885, the New and Latter Day House of Israel. Jezreel's Tower is the temple he planned for his followers. It was to be 120 feet high, with lifts in each of its corner towers, a dome 94 feet in diameter, and a rising platform-pulpit, hydraulically controlled. Thirty thousand pounds were expended and prayers were offered, but the Temple had to be abandoned when it had reached only half its height. The great yellow brick folly, decorated with large bas-reliefs in orange faience tiles of a trumpet with a scroll attached (*The Flying Roll* itself), crossed swords and a crown and the Prince of Wales' feathers, is an astonishing spectacle in its present surroundings of allotments and little villas.

The folly as a form of art is as exclusively English as the Perpendicular style. It is extraordinary that these two extremes, one the perfection of logic, the other the height of unreason, should have been created by the same people. Yet it is possible to make out a case for a national distrust of logic. Many of our parish churches, even of the Perpendicular period, are irregular in plan and picturesque in elevation to a degree unknown abroad. The starry vault of Lincoln leaves function far behind in a flight of fancy that has no parallel in French work of the same date; the lantern of Ely defies logic, and there is more than a hint of the irrational in the exuberant, tropical growth of stone that ripples over the ogee arches of the Lady Chapel. In the folly this impulse is given its head.

[68]

The Triangular Lodge, Rushton,
Northamptonshire, built 1595

Horton Tower, Dorset, seven storeys high,
a landmark for many miles, was built
by Humphrey Sturt, *c.* 1741, as an obser-
vatory, but was never used

The Sham Castle, Wimpole, Cambridgeshire, designed
by Sanderson Miller for Lord Hardwicke, *c.* 1750

Below: The Tattingstone Wonder, Suffolk, three cottages
disguised as a church for Squire White, 1760

Right: Haldon Belvedere or Lawrence
Castle, near Exeter, was built by Sir
Robert Palk in 1788 in memory of his
friend Major-General Stringer Lawrence

A military folly, known as Oliver Ducket, Aske Hall, Yorkshire, built by Sir Conyers D'Arcy

Arno's Castle, Bristol, built by William Reeve, a copper-smelter, of blocks of copper slag, as stables

McCaig's Folly, Oban, was begun by John Stuart McCaig and never completed because its cost exceeded Mr. McCaig's purse. It was intended to be a view-tower and art gallery

[73]

The garden pavilion at Peckover House, Wisbech, Cambridgeshire, built *c.* 1750

On the right: The artificial ruins at Virginia Water, Egham, Surrey, arranged *c.* 1821 for William, Duke of Cumberland

Below: The grotto of tufa, one of the many embellishments of Charles Hamilton's famous Picturesque garden at Pains Hill, Cobham, as it was before it was destroyed

Right: Jezreel's Tower, Gillingham, Kent, 1885

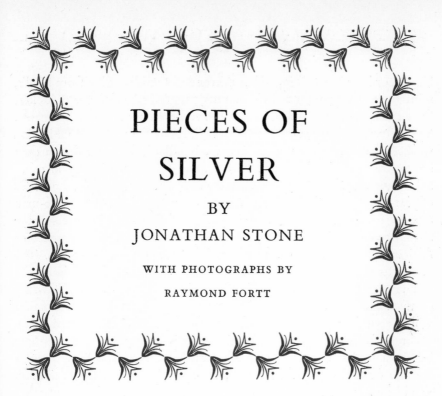

PIECES OF SILVER

BY

JONATHAN STONE

WITH PHOTOGRAPHS BY

RAYMOND FORTT

I T IS a strange non-comprehending look that crosses people's faces when the collecting of antique silver is mentioned. 'Oh, you collect silver, do you? I don't know how you remember all those marks; and how do you ever manage to find them in that big book you have?' There are simple answers to both these questions. 'I *don't* remember all those marks' covers the first part of the question; and 'There's an index' is the truthful answer to the second half.

It rarely seems to occur to the questioner that there is art in silver: collectors do not just amass small strips of hall-marks, any more than Chelsea ceramophiles display cut-out red and gold anchors in their cabinets, or connoisseurs of Old Masters hang small signed canvas corners on their walls.

What differentiates silver from other forms of fine art? Because it is intrinsically a precious metal a certain financial aura seemingly surrounds it. Yet such respect for financial value is quite unnecessary: inch for inch a materially worthless piece of china might easily fetch far more than a piece of silver.

In the twentieth century the difference between an Old Master and a

[77]

Opposite: 'Tuck-in' Coffee Pot
by William Shaw and William
Priest, London 1750

Picasso, or between a Chippendale mirror and a modern glass from Heal's, is immediately apparent to even the most untrained and naïve onlooker, for within these artistic ambits there have been dramatic developments. With silver, however, there has been a reproductive tendency which has worked in cycles, so that there is correspondingly less new design than in any other field of fine art. Further, the cycles of mimicry in other fields have been less tight than they are in silver. For example, thousands of years went by before the recurrence, in our own time, of the cave-man type of painting. In silver the simplicity of design which greeted the beginning of the eighteenth century had disappeared before the seventeen-forties were out, and had reappeared by the seventeen-eighties. The heavy rococo forms which came in around 1730 went out by the 'seventies and reappeared before the end of the third decade of the following century. There are few new designs even today (although an explanation will be seen for this later) and if the centre caster of our illustrated group of three were put side by side at a distance with many a modern example it is possible that even the greatest expert would be unable to distinguish the one from the other. Of course, on closer inspection the distinction would be revealed. Patina does not appear in a day.

The human element is dominant in painting, whereas the designer of silver always has to reckon with mechanical forces. The goldsmiths' art was greatly affected by the Industrial Revolution, which, working upon a certain unexplained conservatism, stifled original creative forces in silver design. There is nothing wrong in the frequent reproduction of fine design, but what has happened since the early nineteenth century is reproduction to the exclusion of almost all new thought. For example, in Her Majesty the Queen's personal collection there is a caster of 1824 by Robert Garrard which is a perfect copy of one made by Paul de Lamerie a hundred years before. Only the other week I was shown a delightful set of casters with the remark, 'Of course they're only copies, but don't you think they're splendid?' I was bound to concede that the quality of the design was fine, for they too were copies of Paul de Lamerie originals made two hundred years earlier.

Has the machine age done a service or disservice to silver? It has certainly meant the almost total disappearance of the craftsman-designer. Today there are but tens remaining where there used to be hundreds. As in many trades, there has been a gradual centralization, and the output of modern factory reproduction silverware from the large Sheffield,

Birmingham and London workshops is very great. In recent years also the craftsmen have had to compete against crippling taxes imposed on their wares: the result of this has been that much antique silver has worked out as cheap as—if not cheaper than—modern silver; and, of course, the value of antique silver is enhanced over the years, whereas modern silver just becomes 'second-hand'. That, at any rate, was the position five years ago, though there have recently been some relaxations of tax on modern craftsman-made silver (which, though there is very little of it, can be aesthetically of the highest order).

The price of antique silver is always on the rise in the auction rooms, and consequently in the shops, yet I think it is fair to say that it does not hold the place it should in the antique field, *vis-à-vis* paintings, china, and furniture. There is an obvious distinction between silver and paintings: silver, for the most part, is made for use; paintings are made for 'looks' —hence their ascendancy in the fine art hierarchy. Silver may have superior intrinsic value to clay, but china is by nature brittle and breakable, whereas silver can be subjected to a good deal of rough treatment without too much detrimental effect. Really fine usable antique china is, in consequence, scarcer than its equivalent in silver.

Although furniture is comparatively fragile, it can be successfully repaired. How, therefore, to account for the fantastically high valuation of fine furniture as against comparable collectors' pieces of silver? The answer seems to lie in education and tradition. What child has not heard of Chippendale? He is almost as prominent in the history books as Macadam or Watt or George Stephenson. Yet you will rarely find a child who has heard of Paul de Lamerie or Paul Storr. There is, in fact, not nearly sufficient emphasis in the schools on the fine and applied arts other than painting and architecture. Indeed it is difficult to think of any English names, apart from Wedgewood and the furniture trio—Chippendale, Hepplewhite and Sheraton—who stand in public estimation anywhere near the congregations of painters, from Hogarth to Augustus John, and architects, from Inigo Jones to Lutyens.

In the eighteenth century—the 'golden age' of the silversmith, if it may be so described—silver found its way into the houses of people of taste and substance, just as paintings, china, and furniture did, and it was highly valued. The order books of the famous silversmiths and the Treasury lists for the Royal Households bear this out. Today, in my opinion, the general estimation of fine antique English silver—and in

consequence, its general price level—is much lower than its aesthetic merits deserve. It would seem to me to offer great opportunities to the intelligent collector.

How, though, does this 'collecting intelligence' develop? The clean, simple designs and the heavily contrasting elaborate decoration each have their firm adherents, but it is the texture of silver that above all provides the attraction and yearning for appreciation and study. Few will pretend that a full understanding of silver is easily acquired. It is, though, a compelling study. The texture of the silver metal lends itself to the most delicate treatment, and how delightful is the warmth of the colour and patina created by years of cleaning and handling—an effect never to be produced by machine.

Silver can be cast or beaten, engraved or chased, and innumerable pieces reflect the affectionate treatment of the craftsmen. Eighteenth-century silver had an 'expression' which moves the collector today. One 'grows accustomed to the face' of a Schuppe cow: she stands and stares appealingly—quite in contrast to the stubborn squatness of a little 'pitcher-cream'. Every piece of silver reflects a mood, and a feeling for this mood is the first sign of intelligence of silver.

A little study and a lot of handling of fine old pieces of silver smooth out a large number of the ruffles in collecting. Silver is primarily a visual art, tempered only incidentally by mundane attention to hall-marks. There are those who consider that a regard for hall-marks on English silver detracts from the visual appreciation, but, when English silver is the only silver in the world in any sense of the words 'fully marked', it would seem sheer folly to ignore the importance of marks. In themselves, they provide an interesting study and they combine powerfully with the brilliant aesthetic attraction of silver form and colour and texture and design to provide an applied art form of unrivalled force.

Acknowledgments

The Warwick cruet and one caster kindly loaned for photography by A. B. Gilbert (Belfast), one cream-jug by Tessiers Ltd., and the coffee-pot and one caster by Walter H. Willson Ltd.

This straight-sided caster of 1664 shows a number of characteristics of the period, such as the 'cut-card' decoration on its cover

Within the first decade of the eighteenth century the straight-sided caster was superseded by the pyriform type, as seen here (*opposite*) exemplified by one of 1712 by Anthony Nelme, a London maker of the highest order. The piercing on the domed cover is exquisite in its simplicity. The vase-shaped caster on a foot appeared in the 1720's, and it is basically that form which has since predominated. Starling Wilford—a specialist caster-maker—made the earliest of the group above (*left*) in 1729. He and his contemporary, Thomas Bamford, tooled very similar products within the somewhat narrow sphere of this austere form. The shapes of both the Nelme and Wilford casters were made in octagonal as well as circular cross-section. By 1750 casters had taken on a more elegant line than that found previously. The one by John Delmester of 1761 (*centre*) has an undulating 'belly' and is far more elaborate, with its rope decoration, intricately pierced cover, and twirling finial. Tall, slim elegance was the key-note for casters made in the Adam period, many of which were made of thin, factory-stamped parts. The light-weight example of 1786 (*right*) reveals such characteristics.

[83]

The small 'pitcher-cream' of 1723 by James Smith, *opposite* (*bottom, centre*), was the earliest form of cream-jug, soon to be joined by the heavy, cast 'nautilus-shell' type represented (*above*) by an example of 1721 by Isaac Liger. The pyriform jug of 1746 by Daniel Piers on three hoof feet, *opposite* (*bottom, left*), was the design which succeeded the small 'pitcher-cream'. A peculiarity to Ireland is the helmet-shaped jug, *opposite* (*bottom, right*) on lion-mask and paw feet, made by William Townsend in *c*. 1753. A dog and a snake are seen on the handles of the two jugs by Samuel Meriton (*top, left and right*) of 1757 and 1759. Phillips Garden's leaf-and-insect jug of 1761 (*top, centre*) rests on a snake-and-vine foot. John Schuppe's 195-year-old cow (*centre*) *disertissime ipsa loquitur*.

The Scotsman Robert Adam studied for a number of years in Southern Italy —primarily at Pompeii and Herculaneum—before coming to settle in London in 1761. Much of the design in the English home for half a century and more following that date reflects the influence of those studies. Silver showed itself particularly amenable to fashioning in the simple lines of this neo-classicism, which is characterized mainly by the minimum of decoration. The Bateman family—consisting of Hester, Peter, Anne, Jonathan, and William—all worked during this period, and the quality of some of their work reaches a high standard. Silver from the workshop of Hester is very popular in the United States, where there are even Bateman Clubs. The hot-water jug (*left*), by Hester, bearing the hallmark for 1785-6, illustrates the finest execution of a supremely classical design. The tea-pot and stand by Peter and Anne Bateman (*above*) show similar clean features. Neither the jug nor the tea-pot is of any great weight, since the gauge of metal used in the second half of the eighteenth century was much finer than that used in the first half, for which change the machine age with its greater efficiency was mainly responsible.

[87]

Casters were grouped in frames, as were oil and vinegar bottles; but not before the appearance of the Warwick cruet—illustrated here by one of 1746 by Samuel Wood—were they all assembled in a single frame

THE FLICKS

BY

J. J. CURLE

NOWADAYS the cinema is just a building, just a pleasure. When I first went inside one it was *the* building, *the* pleasure. At that age what one demanded was size, impressiveness, novelty, glitter—and the cinema had them all. When I was young there were two cinemas within reach of my home. One was considered 'all right' by my mother, but the other showed better films. It was a great day for me when the idea caught on of having a girl walk round spraying disinfectant. After that I could take my pick.

At first, I must admit, the actual performances seen in these buildings rather beat me. Those langorous ladies and gentlemen seemed to be going through such a lot, so slowly, that I simply couldn't get the hang of the plots at all. I remember one—I think it took place in Mexico, or it may have been Spain—anyway, there were white churches with odd steeples on parched hillsides, and the men wore sideburns. The leading man had somehow got tied to the clapper of the local church bell and the heroine had to stop him being deafened, if not totally incapacitated, when the ringers started work. We kept on getting a glimpse of him and then a glimpse of the heroine looking anguished (no one dares look as anguished as that now), and then peeps all round the place: ringers, bell-ropes, church door. Every now and then we would get a view out through the hole in the belfry where the sound usually came from. This seemed to me terribly pointless. The hero obviously wasn't interested in scenery

just then, and, anyway, judging by the way he was lashed to the bell, he would have seen the view upside-down. What happened after that is vague. Probably I had to be taken out because I felt sick—it quite often happened. Maybe the film was just too long.

The first film I almost sat through was *Beau Geste*; but I simply couldn't bear to see Ronald Colman go up in flames, even though the villain had duly been laid across someone's feet, as a dog. Colman was so utterly *decent*. Lifting up my voice I howled and was led out.

We used to go walks in crocodile at school, and getting an interesting partner was always tricky. Yet the term after I saw *The First Girl in the Moon* I had them queuing up. That bit where the expedition is all ready to return and then the villain puts a shot through an oxygen tank and one of the 'good' characters has to stand down—we used to gasp over it together.

But school also had its own films. Every Saturday evening in the winter the whole fifty of us were collected in the senior classroom to watch Felix and Chaplin shorts. At least that's how it seemed then. I now realize that they were only the gilding on a pill of educational single-reelers. I used to enjoy the whole show enormously, especially a vivid cartoon demonstration of the workings of a cow's multiple stomachs in which, through a peculiar streak of prurience, the artist made the final product leave the cow by travelling right down through the length of its tail.

But what really stuck in my mind was Chaplin. I can still remember whole scenes—not perhaps precisely as they took place on the screen, yet with a vividness, a coherence, that is proof of their original impact. The whiffling moustache, the uneasy side-glances, the elaborate lifting of the coat-tails before sitting down on the chair which so often contrived not to be there, the little jerky movements of the stick spreading to an all-over twitching of the body that the nervous graciousness of the smile and the ritual lifting of the hat could not altogether offset; these and the sheer poker-faced, dancing-marionette quality of the man filled me with an admiring joy that was only much later to blend with affection.

We all tried to handle a stick as he did, but not a movement told. How wonderful then to come, years later, at a time when that Chaplin seemed dead for ever, on those electric moments in *Sunset Boulevard*, when Gloria Swanson recaptured it all, down to the very jellification of the legs.

[90]

Still, I was only a schoolboy then, and though I could *sense* the timing I *saw* the custard pies—and I saw the Baron receive them. Whether the Baron figured in many Chaplin shorts I have no idea; but there he stands, in all those I remember, slowly scooping custard pie from his eye-sockets.

It was the slowness that made it perfect, that and the dignity. Yet with him the dignity had a shoddy quality, he mouthed too much, his clothes looked as though they had been hired. For the real thing I had to wait to see Margaret Dumont bridling ecstatically at the sallies of Groucho Marx, an aristocratic rock of ages dissolving to tight-laced blancmange at the resounding tinkle of his advances.

'Just run round her with the tape measure. No, I'll hold the tape measure; you run round her.' The insults fly, and she bridles—the equine metaphor is so exact one has to return to it—she 'backs down', carrying all before and behind her. And then the outrageous compliment: 'Remember the night I drank champagne from your slipper—four quarts,' and she is won. Yet though she is swept off her feet she is never quite carried away. She is, in the last resort, too monumental to vacate her plinth even for Groucho.

I first saw Margaret Dumont in the Cosmo at Cambridge, a place with the glamour of all things unusual and vaguely down-at-heel. In its dark corner, with the solitary lamp casting a half-light round the entrance, it waited there in the frequent fenland mists like a scene from one of its own films—*The Informer* or *Quai des Brumes*, perhaps, or *Sous les Toits de Paris*. Looking up from the damp pavement in front of its doors one half-expected each shiny mackintosh to herald Michele Morgan, or waited for the eerie whistle of a departing steamer to echo from the Cam.

Yet the cinemas I knew first, though little better, seemed anything but shoddy. The square entrance, the illuminated name, the row of scenes-from-the-film displayed in what was obviously the window of a bought-up shop next door, all were accepted as uncritically as the echoing carpetless stairs, with the door marked, undenominationally, 'lavatory', that faced you at the first turn.

Each visit was a ritual, beginning after lunch with a telephone call to a friend or two asking if they would 'feel like the flicks' that evening. If they were free they came. If they were already going, one joined their party. No one ever refused without the most urgent of reasons. Our seats were booked by telephone. There was no need to look up the

number of the cinema or to know it. The name was enough for the local exchange.

When we arrived we would be shepherded down to our places, nodding around to friends. My father would take the seat next the gangway so that he could stretch his legs if he got cramp. Then the lights would dim.

Always there was a Western, and a Trailer that wasted no time on tricks with titling but got down to telling you the story up to some point of enormous suspense. There was the News; often there was a Cartoon—and there was Variety. Harry Lauder made you laugh and cry; Teddy Brown floated his enormous bulk lightly around behind his xylophone; that brilliant white-faced French mime, Sherkot, sailed effortlessly through his apache dance with an imaginary partner. There was nothing cinematic about them, and many of the items were trashy, but we saw, nevertheless, some of the finest stage turns of the day straightforwardly transposed to the screen.

Then came the Big Picture, or rather the big names. For we went to the cinema then to see the Stars. We knew nothing of directors, movements, or social significance, and cared little for plausibility in the plot. What we wanted was to be moved, caught up, transported, whether by laughter or tears or the sheer beauty of virtuosity didn't much matter. We wanted to be amazed, to feel big, to live tremendously. If it was wish-fulfilment it still seems to me better than much of the death-wish-fulfilment, the living-down to what is most commonplace in us that has succeeded it on so many screens. Maybe it was just that we missed the messages and enjoyed the entertainment. Certainly we enjoyed ourselves more obviously. We laughed in the cinema then, just as we laughed in the theatre. We laughed so loud we missed quite a lot of the jokes; presumably their timing was worked out for more sophisticated audiences.

After the show, going home in the car, we pestered our elders with: 'Did you see how he . . . ?' and 'But wasn't it marvellous the way she . . .' It was all so foreign and strange, and unlike anything we lived. Today, with television and the American way of life spreading over the whole western world, nothing can be at once as understandable and appealing, yet at the same time as alien and bizarre, as Hollywood seemed to us then.

If we were a generation of children protected from life at too many points, we were brought up by the cinema as children should be; our heroes behaved heroically, if in over-simplified conventions; the villains never got away with it in the end.

And what pleasing villains they were. The real-life business of compromise had not yet blurred their outlines. From the moment you saw
the long, twisted, Indian-hard face of John Carradine, the suave astrin-
gency of George Sanders, the jovial blackguardism of Akim Tamiroff,
or the oily heavy-lidded shrinkings and shufflings of Peter Lorre, you
knew exactly where you were. You could be quite sure they wouldn't
make one decent gesture till the picture ended, unless you counted a
forcefully extorted death-bed confession. Of course, even here there
were the exceptions, the Humphrey Bogarts and Joseph Calleias and
Paul Lukases, who would suddenly show the man peering out, half
terrified, half insane with pride, from inside the murderer as he stood
there without a movement.

The heroes, too, could become equivocal, as in the spidery run of
Burgess Meredith's breaking into *Idiot's Delight*, fiery with a pacifism we
should like to have trusted in those Munich days, yet unable in his honesty
to hide that what he was offering was that people should suffer rather than
that they should triumph.

But usually virtue seemed so agreeable. Ronald Colman was just
exactly that nice army major with whom your father went duck-shooting,
and Clark Gable the obvious man to whom to trust untold gold, if not
perhaps 'the ladies of the party'.

Now, for a few years, the two strains of heroes, the 'toughs' and the
'lovers', the Fairbanks and the Valentinos, were to come nearer together
than ever before or afterwards. At least twice the perfect fusion was
achieved, in Robert Donat and Leslie Howard, when staggering good
looks were combined with obviously inflexible courage and a deadly,
elegantly used wit. Looking back over a waste of love-scenes—passionate,
grandiose, 'spiritual', or plain silly—the two that stand out still in my
memory are two vignettes: Robert Donat's mountain interlude with
Greer Garson in *Goodbye, Mr Chips*, and Leslie Howard's few words with
Mary Morris in *Pimpernel Smith* about the postcard of the Venus de
Milo. Both are such fragments of everyday living as provide almost
accidentally our great moments. Both depend on absolute sincerity.
That they also lend themselves easily to caricature is the price that often
has to be paid for the best.

For the steadily maintained level of dead-on-the-mark, one-hundred-
per-cent success one had to turn to the good 'bit' player, and here the
'thirties were peculiarly rich. From the grand old English aristocrat of

C. Aubrey Smith, via the butler of Eric Blore or Arthur Treacher, right through to the plump squeaky-voiced put-upon cowboy of Andy Devine, there was hardly a type, male or female, for which one could not take one's pick amongst a number of equally talented contenders. The lines they were given were often far from brilliant, but they 'came over' because these people were genuine 'humours'. Donald Meek looking like the one at a chimps' tea-party who never manages to get at the food; Marjorie Main, arms akimbo, answering back in God-fearing frontiersman style; Claude Dampier drooling away, vague, round-shouldered, but infinitely hopeful, at the blackboard in Will Hay's over-comprehensive school—all played parts which did not seem to have been written but merely to be excerpts from real lives which must continue off-stage between pictures.

Economically the bit player's standing was sound, because his fortunes did not rise and fall like those of the stars. Many, like Paul Lukas and Adolphe Menjou, had known stardom in their younger days and were to know it again. Many were given the chance of bigger things in the occasional film that suited their talents, and some of these performances, like Akim Tamiroff's as the surgeon-lecturer in *Disputed Passage*, were brilliant.

But it was as their 'second selves' that we really knew them, waiting for them with the contentment that the familiar brings when it has got beyond being trite to being true. How we welcomed Harry Davenport's eternally jaunty, eternally adolescent-hearted cracker-barrel philosophers and Frank Morgan's grandiloquent gone-to-seed heavy fathers and con-men. How relieved we were when the chairmanship of the meeting during the vital session lay in the strong hands of Edward Arnold, or when the judgment that was to free the innocent victim was given by Lewis Stone. The traffic always seemed to run more smoothly for the presence of Pat O'Brien's warm brogue and the course of musical true love more delightfully when chaperoned by many-chinned S. Z. 'Cuddles' Zakall's Austrian-accented benignity.

No kitchen or camp-fire had a cook who brought the smell of frying chips to the nostrils like Henry Armetta, with his enormous round face, curly springing hair, and tiny, pursed-up sipping lips. And, in the days when Russians were still only the melancholy Slavs of the post-war night-club, who could switch so devastatingly from mood to mood as Mischa Auer with his bloodhound devotion and angular but impeccable

manners? In an age, too, when women had finally won the domination of the American scene, there were unrivalled opportunities for the actor of shrinking dismay, perhaps the best of them being that quivering mad-hatter of apology, Edward Everett Horton, closely followed by Hugh Herbert and that most tetchy yet indomitable ulcer-sufferer, Eugene Pallette.

In England the bit player never came into his own to the same extent. English eccentricity runs less to surface mannerisms than the American article, and is often characterized by an under-emphasis that needs elbow room to make its effects. Background players we had in plenty, especially police officers and plain-clothes men of the Anthony Holles, Edward Chapman stamp. But the humour that the bit players supplied in America we got from secondary stars like Gordon Harker, Francis L. Sullivan, Basil Radford, and Naunton Wayne, players who created a character and stuck to it almost unchanged throughout their film careers.

Undoubtedly the finest of the eccentrics on this side of the Atlantic—and never finer than in some of his early appearances as a dyspeptic newspaper editor—was Alistair Sim, one of the few actors who really understands the meaning and the pronunciation of the verb 'to gibber'.

How often, looking back, it is some line spoken or some gesture sketched by one of these subsidiary figures that sticks in the mind when everything else about a film has vanished from the memory: Joseph Calleia as Inspector Slimane saying of Pepe-le-Moko in *Algiers*: 'I have marked the date of his arrest there on the wall, high up, but it reads red in the light of the setting sun;' or the voice—I cannot put a face to it—murmuring confidentially in *Top Hat*: 'I understand that he buys her all her niceties, and her niceties are *very* nice.' What a gallery of bit players just those two films provided. Add *You Can't Take It With You* and there's almost enough to start a casting directory.

Yet in *Algiers* I think that for once the honours for the single clinching line that creates a character in the round must go to one of the stars, Hedy Lamarr, the most statically perfect beauty ever to appear on the screen. Married (or was it only engaged—or worse? How vague one gets) to an unprepossessing man twice her age, she is explaining to a friend the benefits of this arrangement, especially in the matter of dress. The friend, eager to know more of her background, asks: 'And what did you do before you had these clothes?' To which she replies with a deadly veracity: 'I wanted them!'

[95]

In the final reckoning, however, it was not the brilliant bit player, the fine character actor, or even the star that made the greatness of the films of the 'thirties; it was the *phenomena*. Everyone will have his own candidates for the gallery of these players who were more than life-size, legendary in all they did. For me there are six who qualify, with three very near misses.

The near misses first: toad-like yet sensitive Edward G. Robinson, James Cagney, the tireless 'trouper', and that most moving of off-beat actresses, Katharine Hepburn. Then two 'phenomena' I never saw, the invisible Walt Disney and Mae West, inspiration of more (if less publicly quoted) stories than Aberdeen or the Model T Ford. Next, Dietrich and Garbo; and finally, head and shoulders above all competitors for sheer acting ability and dramatic impact, Spencer Tracy and Bette Davis.

The last two years of the 'thirties took me to Cambridge and into the army as they were taking the country through Munich and into a war. The pace changed; styles of living and thinking and acting changed. The unemphatic, basically peasant-culture world of the French film, with its sudden fierce outbursts of emotion and sharp, open-eyed humour, destroyed belief—as it seemed, for ever—in the 'entertainments' of Hollywood. The films of Raimu, Jouvet, Jean Gabin, Françoise Rosay, Harry Baur, Pierre Blanchar, and Fernandel led logically to the wartime mixture of dedicated high drama and homely humour of which John Mills and Celia Johnson showed so well the active and the passive sides. Then, after the triple irruption of Laird Cregar, Orson Welles, and Van Heflin, the actor seemed for a time almost to disappear behind the machine, lost in semi-fictionalized documentaries.

When entertainment came back something had changed. Humour had turned into the wisecrack or the platitude. We had grown up, or the recipes had been overworked. Now the great films were half fantasy, but it was a directionless fantasy without hope, worlds away from the Capra touch.

The pilot's hallucinations as he 'flew' the junked bomber in *The Best Years of Our Lives*, Barrault's stricken clown swamped in the crowd at the end of *Les Enfants du Paradis*, the sub-acid cut-and-thrust of *All About Eve*—these were the images of a world that had learned certain things it had no means of forgetting. Von Stroheim, organizing the great actress's departure to her trial for murder in *Sunset Boulevard*, as though it were just another superb film exit, announced the end of that world of

Top Hat (B.B.C.). Fred Astaire and Ginger Rogers in one of their languidly precise romantic routines

The Gold Rush (United Artists). Chaplin, the little man whose girl didn't come to dinner

Le Jour Se Lève (National Film Archive). Jean Gabin and Arletty in a sad French film that made 'love' an adult matter in the cinema

Animal Crackers (Paramount). Groucho Marx and Margaret Dumont. 'If you won't entertain my proposal, just entertain me'

Beau Geste (Paramount). Ronald Colman and Ralph Forbes prepare to do 'the right thing' in their Foreign Legion outpost

You Can't Take It With You (Columbia). The ponderous meet the pixilated. *Left to right:* Spring Byington, Lionel Barrymore, Jean Arthur, James Stewart, Mary Forbes, and Edward Arnold

Goodbye, Mr Chips (M.G.M.). The awkwardness of first avowals. Robert Donat and Greer Garson, marooned on the mountain

Algiers (United Artists). On the left are Joseph Calleia and Hedy Lamarr, the temptress. On the right is Charles Boyer as Pépé le Moko, lonely master of the Casbah

Opposite: A Hundred Men and a Girl (National Film Archive). Mischa Auer, Deanna Durbin, and Adolphe Menjou in a fairy-tale film of youth triumphant, only equalled in charm by *Meet Me in St Louis*

Pimpernel Smith (British National). Leslie Howard and Mary Morris, players whose intelligence and timing allowed them to show 'restraint' as a positive force

Captains Courageous (M.G.M.). Freddie Bartholomew, Lionel Barrymore, and Spencer Tracy aboard a Grand Banks schooner

Sunset Boulevard (Paramount). Eric von Stroheim 'directs' Gloria Swanson's final exit— as a murderess

The African Queen (Independent Film Distributors). Katharine Hepburn and Humphrey Bogart. The once-prim mission lady thaws on the long river trip to safety

expensive illusions to which he had himself contributed with unique lavishness.

Later, from disillusion came specialization; more vivid horror, more explicit sex, more emphatic sadism—the Brando-Bardot treatment. For a time the French held out—*Monsieur Vincent, Les Belles de Nuit,* and Tati—then they, too, were swept away on the tide.

To the man of forty it proverbially seems that all the best things have happened; yet the change cannot be entirely imaginary. Cinemas close; people turn to television. And the thing on television at which even the children laugh out loud is—the cinema comedy of the 'thirties.

So perhaps no one really *has* pushed up his spectacles like Leslie Howard, or whispered like Colman, or smoked like Bogart, or smiled like Hepburn, or puzzled like Tracy, or frozen like Garbo, or crooned like Crosby, or danced like Astaire, or kissed like Boyer, or grinned like Gable, or leered like Laughton, or carolled like Durbin, or trouped like Temple, or gangled like Stewart, or goggled like Cantor, or beamed like Benchley, or swum like Weismuller. Perhaps the 'thirties really were the golden age of cinema *entertainment.* At any rate, some of us will go on thinking so, living in a happy, euphoric dream, where, as the mighty Wurlitzer sinks into its pit amidst all the colours of the rainbow, as the 'chocolates, cigarettes' girls scurry for the back of the circle, we see those filmy curtains draw apart for the big picture of the evening, *Top Hat*—and no one has seen it before.

Fanny (National Film Archive). The 'Marseilles' group that is led by Raimu and Charpin in the superb Pagnol trilogy, *Marius, Fanny, César*

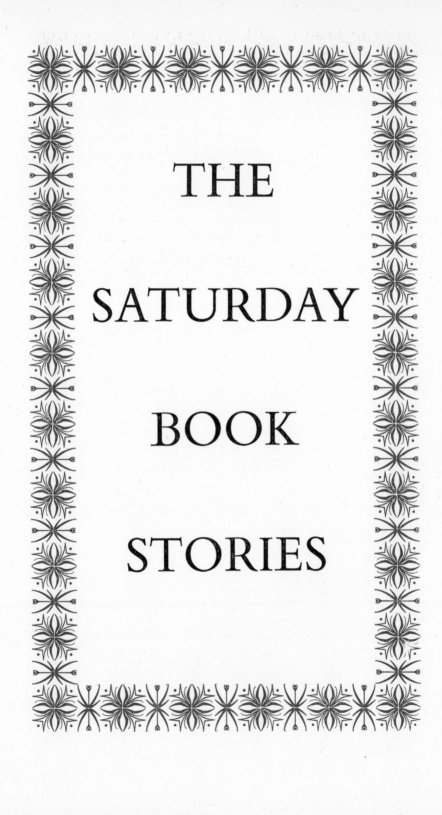

THE

SATURDAY

BOOK

STORIES

THE CATWALK

BY MICHAEL TAAFFE

THAT year Shane joined the Society of the Red Dagger. He had one of those Swedish knives that fold on themselves and fit into the handle. It was attached by a ring to a key-chain that ran from his braces button into his trousers pocket where he could feel it, hard and lumpy, all during class. So when Corcoran took his penny and stamped him on the back of his hand with the rubber stiletto, smeared with indelible ink, he was a full member except for the test.

Shane went around with Legs Duffy and O'Hare. They had knives too—Bushman's Friends in leather sheaths—but Corcoran hadn't taken their pennies. The eyes in O'Hare's long horse-face looked a little smaller and he was very quiet for a while, but he didn't complain. Legs was openly bitter.

'It's your sister, that's what it is!' he told Shane. 'I heard Corcoran sayin' to Baily that she was a lovely mot.'

'Sure, you're always hearin' things,' said Shane comfortably. He looked down at the smudged imprint on his hand.

'An' another thing,' said Legs. 'I know what the test's goin' to be this time.'

'What?' said the other two at once.

'I'm not tellin',' said Legs, 'but it'll take a good man to do it.'

They were sitting in the lee of a hedge bordering Harmony Lane that was a short-cut on the way home from school.

O'Hare rummaged in his satchel and brought out a small tin box from which he produced a frayed cigarette. 'Would you like a draw?' he invited, addressing himself pointedly to Shane.

Legs watched while O'Hare lit up. He puffed hard until the burning tobacco glowed brightly, inhaled deeply, and, holding his breath, muttered, 'Hello, kid!' before releasing the smoke. His eyes watered and he was shaken by a cough as he passed the cigarette to Shane. 'Bit of a cold,' he gasped and relapsed into another fit of coughing.

Shane handled the cigarette expertly. Blowing on the lighted end he looked sideways at Legs.

[107]

'A smoke's a great thing for warmin' you up, I think,' he said, and took a puff.

'Oh, all right!' grunted Legs. 'It's the big wall down at the Pigeon House—the one between the two red-brick buildings. Y'have to go across the catwalk at the top. Now, gimme the fag!'

'How d'ye know?' said O'Hare, as Shane passed the cigarette to Legs.

'Sure, Marais told me,' said Legs amid clouds of smoke. 'He's well in with Corcoran. The test's on Saturday.'

'On Saturday!' cried Shane. He tried to sound casual.

There was a silence.

He'd never do it, Shane knew. He'd fall for certain. Sure, halfway up the iron ladder let into the wall had been enough to make him tired and giddy, the time they'd all been down there in the summer. Just because he wanted to be like the others he was always pushing himself forward, and now look where it had got him! Sure, the top of the wall must be——

'Marais hasn't done it yet,' said Legs with relish.

'Oh, Marais. . . .' sniffed O'Hare. 'Those fecking South Africans'll do anything for notice. Did you see'm at the match on Saturday? Tacklin' chaps twice his size round the ankles—he'll get himself laid out!'

'He's not worth his place!' pronounced Legs.

'He is so!' contradicted Shane. 'He's the best half-back we've had since the year we beat Belvedere!'

'Who says so?' demanded Legs.

'Corcoran says so! I heard him talking to Father Matt, an' that's what he said!'

'You'd believe anything Corcoran said, now that he's taken your penny!' shouted Legs. 'Wouldn't you?'

He looked at O'Hare for corroboration.

'Well, now,' murmured O'Hare diplomatically, 'I wouldn't say that Marais isn't a *good* player. A bit of a shaper, maybe——'

'He's not a shaper,' said Shane stubbornly.

'Ah, I'm disgusted with you! Sure I don' know what you see in him,' growled Legs. 'Anyway, I'm off home to me tea. Comin', Hairy?' He rose to his feet.

O'Hare stubbed out the half-smoked cigarette on the sole of his boot and replaced it carefully in the tin box. He strapped his satchel and stood up.

[108]

'I'm going across the field,' said Shane, not moving.

'Oh, well. . . .' O'Hare's voice was gentle. 'See you tomorrow.'

'So long!' muttered Legs.

They went down the lane together, O'Hare with his pointed, dancing-master's walk, Legs moving bandily beside him. At the corner, O'Hare turned and waved. Shane waved back.

It must be sixty—no, a hundred feet, he thought. Maybe more. Who'd chosen *that* for the test? It wasn't fair—and they'd all come down to see, trust them! Sure, the Pigeon House itself gave him the shivers, let alone the test. The mournful hooting of the coal-boats as they came in with the tide on a foggy evening—he could hear it now. And the day the mackerel were in and he'd gone off before breakfast with his father, the two of them on bicycles riding down Sandymount Road, his father carrying the short sea rod in case Shane got it mixed up with his handle-bars. And after the six bullet-shaped slippery fish had been landed, when his father had hooked something heavier than the rod would lift and in it came, turning sluggishly in the dark water until Shane could see the face of the dead woman, greenish with staring eyes below the dirty surface of the water that licked at the slime on the concrete. And when the policeman had come and his father had given his name and address they had thrown the mackerel back in the water and ridden home in silence, Shane furtively eyeing the rod that had brought from the sea the sacklike dripping thing that lay on the breakwater before the policeman had thrown something over it to hide it from sight—any other place but the Pigeon House and maybe he could manage it! He shut his eyes and thought of the height and the strain on his hands going up the ladder. . . .

'H'lo!' said a voice above him.

Shane looked up. His troubles fell away from him. 'H'lo, Marais!' he said eagerly.

'How goes it?' enquired the newcomer, squatting easily beside the smaller boy. His fair skin and tousled corn-blond hair contrasted oddly with the hint of maturity in his blunt features.

'Oh, all right,' said Shane. 'There's something I wanted to know, though. I expect you could tell me.'

'What is it?' asked Marais lazily, turning his wide-set eyes on the other.

'Well, I wanted to know . . .' mumbled Shane. It was suddenly very difficult to say it.

'Come on, then!' said Marais, with a flash of even teeth. 'Spit it out!'

'I just wondered—I mean—how high izit?' ended Shane in a rush.

'How high . . . ? Oh, I see! You mean the test?'

Shane nodded dumbly.

'M-m, let's see now,' murmured Marais. He picked up a stick, pulled a penknife from his pocket, and began to whittle abstractedly.

'All of twenty steps up the ladder—call it twenty feet, I s'pose,' he said at length.

'Twenty feet!' said Shane incredulously. 'But—is *that* all? Only twenty steps up the ladder?'

'Looks more, I know,' nodded Marais. 'These things always look worse than they are. There's nothin' to it. I went across last night.'

'Oh!' breathed Shane. 'A practice, sort of?'

'Well—kind of,' said Marais. 'Don't tell anyone!'

'Oh, no! Oh, no, Marais!' said Shane earnestly.

'There's nothin' to it,' Marais repeated. 'All y'need is a decent balance.' He looked Shane over. 'Not scared, are you?'

'Hell, no!' said Shane contemptuously. He took out his knife, fitted it together, found a twig, and set to whittling busily.

'I don't suppose I'd have as good a balance if it hadn't been for Makok,' Marais said casually.

'Who's Makok?'

'Oh, he was a house-boy we had in Natal—a Zulu. He had friends among the witch-doctors.'

'The witch-doctors?' said Shane. His mouth stayed open.

'Yes. I had a bang on the shin, y'see, an' got a disease called osteo-something. I've got the name written down at home. The doctor had to scrape the bone.'

'Did it hurt?'

'Like blazes! But after it was over Makok came into my room an' said he'd get me a lion-bone.'

'A lion-bone?'

'That's what Makok said. I was young at the time.' He looked appraisingly at Shane. 'Smaller than you, I was.'

'What's a lion-bone?'

'There's a little bone in a lion's shoulder that the hunters always cut out an' keep, for luck. All the Africans know about it. It's a vesti—vesti-something-or-other bone, the sort of bone the lions don't need any more

because their shoulder muscles are so strong. Anyway, Makok said it had magic and that he'd get me one.'

'What for?'

'He said that if I rubbed it over the place on my leg it would heal quicker an' that I'd walk as sure-footed as a cat when I was well.'

'You're not foolin' me?'

'I'm not,' said Marais. He rolled down his stocking. 'There's the scar—you can see for yourself.'

'How big was the bone?' said Shane, sitting back on his haunches.

'It's only a little bone, that would fit in a matchbox. I have it still,' said Marais. 'It was from a lion, but Makok said that all cats have it, leopards an' lynxes an'——'

'Even an ordinary cat—a cat like you have in the house?'

'I think so. Makok said that's why all cats walk the same way. They kind of slink along an' can swipe in any direction with their front legs. They have great balance, too.'

It was true, thought Shane. He had a vision of Rafferty, the cat at home, moving surely and sleekly over the roofs while Shane's sister stood below, calling vainly.

'Did you use the bone?' he asked.

'Bet you I did! I knew Makok wouldn't tell me a lie. I rubbed it on the place every night over the bandage an' afterwards when my leg was better I used to rub it on my shin. Makok said to tell no one. You won't tell, you swear?'

'I swear!' said Shane solemnly.

Marais grunted. 'Wouldn't be fair to Makok,' he explained.

Shane sat quietly, thinking it all over.

'Hell's bells!' exploded Marais, looking down at his penknife. The small blade had caught on a knot in the wood and was broken off short. 'An' the sharp blade, too!' he lamented.

'Oh, bad luck!' cried Shane. 'I——' He stopped suddenly, for a great, a wonderful, idea had come to him.

'I say, Marais!' he said excitedly. 'I say!'

'Uh?' muttered the other, intent on his broken knife.

'Marais!' Shane's voice was filled with an urgency that caught the bigger boy's attention. 'Marais, would you . . .'

'What is it now?' said Marais, looking curiously at the small, flushed face.

[111]

'Listen!' said Shane. 'You've always liked my knife, haven't you? Well . . .' he fumbled with the chain, unfastened the knife, and held it out. 'Take it! Please take it!'

'But I couldn't do that, man!' protested Marais.

'Listen—please listen t'me!' begged Shane. '*Please* take the knife! You can have it—I want you to have it! An'——'

'Ah, now, look here——'

'Wait a minnit! Please listen!' broke in Shane, all his diffidence swept away by the magnitude of his idea. 'I want—would you, please, lend me the bone as a swap—the lion-bone? Just a lend! I won't tell a soul! Will you? Oh, Marais, please!'

Palpitating, he waited for the answer.

'It wouldn't be fair,' said Marais uneasily. 'The bone's old an'—an' dried up now. Maybe it's no good any more. I couldn't take——'

'Oh, but *please*! Just for a few days! I want it! Do this for me an' I'll never forget!' entreated Shane. 'Bring it to school tomorrow! Say you will, Marais!'

'Well,' relented Marais, 'if that's the way you want it, but I tell you——'

'Oh, thanks—thanks very much! You *will* bring it? Give it t'me before class, will you? I'll be at the bottom of the big stairs! You promise, don't you, Marais?'

'I'll bring it,' promised Marais, 'but I don't think . . .'

Already on his feet, Shane gulped hurriedly. 'Must go, 'm late! An' thank you very, very much! See you t'morrow!' He hitched on his satchel and squeezed through the hedge, leaving Marais sitting with the knife in his hand.

' 'Bye—see you t'morrow!' he called cheerfully.

' 'Bye!' Marais answered.

Shane moved slowly across the field. Inside his pocket he gripped the end of his key-chain firmly in a moist hand. It would be all right now, he knew. Once let him get the bone and he'd use it regularly—maybe three times a day and he'd soon be able for the test. Perhaps Corcoran would put it off for a bit, until he was really ready. He'd ask him.

It would be all right, it would be all right, sang his hammering heart. His foot in its surgical boot dragged a little as he picked his way over the furrows, borne on the wings of imagination and moving with the insolent, balanced, rubbery walk of a cat.

The Letter

BY OLIVE COOK

Miss Louisa Hopper had been a confirmed invalid since she had almost died of scarlet fever at the age of sixteen. Soon after that time Milly Brunton had come to live at Eldon Lodge. Milly, a distant relative, had been left a penniless orphan, and Mrs Hopper had been only too glad to take her in, for it was a relief to have someone who would sit with poor Louisa and bear with the whims and complaints which of course she could not help. Years went by. Mr and Mrs Hopper had both passed away and Louisa's sister Deborah had long since been married to the solicitor Arthur Fosbrooke, but Milly was still at Eldon Lodge, the indispensable companion of Louisa.

One July afternoon the two ladies were sitting in the garden. Mrs Fosbrooke, who lived nearby, was expected for tea, and Hetty, the maid, was measuring out the drops prescribed by Dr Richardson to calm Louisa's nerves when she had to endure the strain of visitors. Milly was reading aloud to her the opening chapter of Mr Charles Garvice's latest novel *Just a Girl*, which had come that morning from Mudie's.

Louisa's drops had hardly taken effect when Deborah arrived, wearing a smart new bonnet and gown and clearly rather excited. Without waiting to hear Louisa's answer to a perfunctory inquiry after her health she said: 'There's something I want to tell you. Arthur brought home a copy of the *Suffolk Chronicle* yesterday; he was advertising in it on behalf of a client. I happened to glance through it when I saw an announcement that Mr Hugh Atherton, of The Priory, West Stowe, had died in Ceylon. You two have perhaps forgotten him,' she went on with a meaning glance at Milly, 'but I have often thought of him. He rowed for King's and used to bicycle over from Cambridge when we were staying with the McKendricks at Clayhithe.

'Do you remember that afternoon when Sarah, Florence, Isobel, and I walked along the towpath with Professor McKendrick to look for milkweed and Swallow-tail butterflies? You, Milly, had of course been left behind in case Louisa should need you.

'It was very hot for the end of May, and we sat down by the river. Sarah was nearly asleep, but I said I would see whether there were any Swallow-tails in the next meadow.

'I walked round the river bend where the towpath ended, and I was just climbing the stile into Ditton fields when I caught sight of a light dress, a boat, and the figure of a man. I recognized the dress at once. It was my last year's pink muslin that I had given to you, Milly Brunton. And there were you alone with Mr Atherton. Surely you aren't blushing after all these years? But of course you have never suspected that anyone saw you. I was stunned. I had never seen Mr Atherton pay you any particular attention. In fact I was sure he was partial to me. You were always sitting with Louisa when he called, and you were not with us at the Ball when he asked me for three dances and took me in to supper.

'I drew nearer, keeping behind the willows. I heard Mr Atherton say, "It would be a great pleasure, Miss Brunton, if you would let me row you up to the Pike and Eel for tea; you won't be away more than an hour; you will be back before the girls."

' "Indeed, Mr Atherton," you replied. "I ought never to have left Louisa. It is kind of you to ask me, but I must go back; I said I would not be gone more than half an hour."

'I could not hear his answer, but I saw you climb out of the boat. Mr Atherton stepped into it as you got out, seized you by the hand, and tried to pull you down beside him. You tried to disengage your hand and cried out, "Please, please, Mr Atherton; I never would have thought it of you; I won't be trifled with, though I am only a poor orphan."

'You ran towards the towpath with Mr Atherton after you, and he soon caught up with you. You were too far away for me to hear what he said, but I could see that his face was very red and you were crying. In a minute or two he strode off. You stood where he left you and I had to jump two ditches to get back to the others without being seen.

'I said nothing about what I had seen. Mr Atherton called the following afternoon while you were upstairs with Louisa. He stayed much longer than usual and sat most of the time with me. He asked after Louisa but did not mention you. He said he would be leaving Cambridge in a day or two and going down to his home in Suffolk, but hoped to call again before that. But we did not see him again. I watched you, Milly, but you looked and behaved as you always did. About a week later I was strolling towards the house past the stables and the groom's cottage when I saw Mark the postman talking to one of the maids. I offered to take the letters up to the house. There was only one, a thick cream envelope. It bore a Suffolk postmark and it was addressed to you, Milly.

'I remember I was so shocked I hardly knew what I was doing. The letter was only very lightly stuck down and before I knew what I was about I had opened it. I saw at once what was in it. It began "My dearest Miss Brunton" and was a proposal from Mr Atherton to you, Milly. I do assure you it was so, though you may well find it hard to believe, as I still do. I know it's wrong to open other people's letters, but by the time I had reached my room and thought it all over calmly I was very glad I had done so in this case. I was quite sure you were not pining for Mr Atherton, and it would only have upset you to receive such a letter. Besides, what should we have done if you had left dear Louisa? It was certainly all for the best that the letter had fallen into my hands, and I kept it. There's no harm in telling you about it now the poor man is dead. In fact, I feel you should have the letter now. Even if you can't remember Mr Atherton, Milly, I feel it will do you good to know you have had at least one proposal in your life.'

(*The photographs were found by Olive Cook in the collection at the Victoria and Albert Museum, by whose courtesy they are here reproduced.*)

CARRY ME BACKWARDS

BY CHRISTOPHER SHORT

I N CENTERVILLE, Virginia, when they are not hunting or riding they are drinking and talking about hunting and riding. I know, because I have quite a few friends there whom I visit occasionally. I have often taken part in the local activities during these fleeting visits. That is to say, I have drunk highballs and talked about riding. Once I actually rode, an experience neither I nor Centerville society are likely to forget.

When everyone else is talking about riding, one must perforce remain silent unless one talks about riding too. As it would have invited social ostracism to confess that I had hardly ever ridden at all, I fell into the habit of talking as if I were quite a horseman, banking on the fact that my visits to Centerville were always brief, seldom lasting more than a few hours, and I could get away before anybody called my bluff. It was really quite easy. I just dropped an occasional remark, usually a true one, like '*I* never use a snaffle', into the conversational pool. This kept me in the swim and made Centervillians feel that I was civilized.

I got caught, however, when I was once so unwise as to accept an invitation to spend a week-end in Centerville. The friends who invited me are called George and Mary Dexter. They are very Virginian types, although George was born and bred in Westchester County, New York, and Mary comes from Cape Cod. Still, it is wonderful what a little Virginia air will do to one's accent, and George and Mary are indistinguishable from the rest of the Centervillians, many of whom, as a matter of fact, come from other States too.

George is in his mid-thirties and red-faced. Mary is a few years younger and she doesn't need to use rouge either. Both have that bow-legged charm that comes from a long association with horses. George and I were at school together. We have the type of close friendship that often springs from a long mutual antipathy. Not that I really dislike George. As I say, he has some very attractive qualities to those who like horses.

The other guests were very much like George and Mary. That is the best and the worst that can be said of them. The household resembled a large, luxurious stable filled with hearty equines addicted to fermented oats.

I arrived on Saturday afternoon in time for tea. Of course no one in Centerville ever drinks tea, but to say that I arrived in time for a glass of Bourbon could mean that I got there at any hour of the day.

We had a fine time Saturday evening sitting around drinking and talking about riding. We had a fine time Sunday morning doing the same thing. A blonde filly, who looked as if she might bite me at any minute, took rather a shine to me, and I am ashamed to say that in view of her obvious interest I did more boasting than I should have done.

She asked me if I did a lot of riding. I replied truthfully that most of my riding had been done out West. This was quite true, for I had done no riding in the East at all. I *had*, however, once ridden a horse while visiting a dude ranch. It had been a distasteful experience for both of us, and I had walked home. For exercise thereafter I played checkers with the manager of the ranch, who couldn't ride either.

She wanted to know if I hunted. I responded with less truth, but not entirely inaccurately, that I had hunted in England. What I did not say was that my hunting experiences amounted to following the Heythrop for a short distance in a car.

My girl-friend was very impressed with me. Bourbon was making her less and less inhibited. Not that she had many inhibitions to start with.

'I'd love to see you in your pinks!' she cried, nuzzling my arm. 'I'll bet you're a cutie pie.'

This struck me as being a bit forward, but I was not to be outdone and said I'd bet she'd look pretty nice in hers too, whether they were pink, blue, green, or just plain white with lace trimmings. I felt that perhaps I had gone a bit too far, but she didn't seem to mind and playfully kicked my shin.

A youth with a crew cut, who looked as if he had spent most of his life falling off horses on to his head, for the top of it was nearly flat, fixed me with that vacant expression which appears to be part of the curriculum of some of the more fashionable Eastern prep schools, and enquired in the carefully non-committal accents of the Ivy League whether I preferred posting English fashion or riding Western style. I realized that his question was prompted by the need of his kind to identify himself with the group in which he found himself rather than because of any wish for information, and I replied jocularly that the thing about posting was one had to have a stamp, whereas all one needed for Western style was a brand. This was well received, and there was a chorus of laughter.

A middle-aged man with the complexion of an over-ripe grape asked me how I had found the animals in England. I responded that the caribou were lousy, but that I took it he was referring to foxes and they were cunning as hell owing to the fact that they had been hunted for so long. I said I'd even heard of a fox pretending to be a hound and helping to chase himself all over the map. He gave me an odd look and said he'd meant horses. Made carefree by Bourbon I replied that the only difference I had observed between English and American horses was that the former used a broad neigh and the latter a short one. His complexion became more grape-like than ever and he retired into his Bourbon glass; but I kept going and soon was the life of the party. I was riding high.

Then George pulled me right down into low by calling out: 'Come on, everybody, let's ride over to Midway before lunch! We can have a drink with the Burgoynes. There are enough horses for everyone.'

George's invitation fairly put the wind up me. Any sort of riding, even on the quietest old nag, would reveal me as the charlatan I was.

'Thanks very much,' I stammered, 'but I can't.'

'Why not?' asked George menacingly. It struck me that he was a bit too anxious for me to come on this ride. I suspected that he was jealous of my social success and wanted to cut me down to size. There was no way he could know how little riding I had done, but he had every reason to suspect that I was not the horseman I had been making myself out to be.

'I really can't,' I said desperately. 'I'm . . . I'm not well.'

By this time everyone was looking at me, and to my fevered imagination it seemed as if suspicion was beginning to dawn in their eyes. It was at high noon in George's.

'What's the matter?' he asked. 'Chicken?'

'Certainly not,' I responded with heat. 'I can ride anything you can.'

'Is that a bet?'

'Sure is,' I said, feeling trapped.

'Ten dollars suit you?'

'Make it fifteen,' I said recklessly.

'O.K.,' said George. 'We'll get Killjoy out. If you can stay on him ten minutes you win the bet.'

'You've got to show that you can ride him, too,' I said.

'I'll get up after you get bucked off,' he replied. 'I can ride him.'

'O.K.,' said I, with as much swagger as I could muster, 'but are you sure it will be a fair test?'

'Why not?'

'Well, for one thing,' I said weakly, 'I haven't brought my saddle.'

'Do you usually when you go visiting?' he asked with real surprise.

'Of course not; but what I mean is you'll be used to the saddle and I won't.'

'You made the bet,' he responded coldly. 'You said you could ride anything I could. I take it that means under any conditions.'

'But I haven't any clothes,' I cried, in a final effort to fend off my doom.

'I'll lend you some. O.K.?'

'O.K.' I gulped down the half glass of Bourbon-on-the-rocks I had intended sipping until lunch-time, and felt better.

George's riding things fitted me quite well. Hoping for the best, I walked out to the front of the house, where horses for the entire party were being brought round.

The name Killjoy exactly suited my steed. He looked as if he wanted to kill anything within reach. He was a large black stallion with the wild and arrogant expression of a Revivalist preacher and the same sinister way of pawing the ground.

I made an excuse, went back into the house, and sneaked another slug of Bourbon. When I came out again the others were all mounted and were waiting for me. A cheer went up when I appeared, weaving slightly, at the door. I set my course gallantly towards the horse.

The groom had a hard time controlling Killjoy, who appeared to take an instant dislike to me and to resent my approach. With a beating heart I prepared to mount.

Here a difficulty presented itself. Whenever I came near him, Killjoy jumped about so much it was impossible for me to get my foot into the stirrup.

'There, there now,' I said placatingly. 'Nice horsey! Good old Killer!' I tried to pat his neck, but he leapt away and left me waving vaguely in his direction as if I were bidding him adieu. Some of the guests evidently thought that was what I was doing and called out to me not to be afraid. Nettled, I determined to show these people what real horsemanship was.

It is remarkable how Bourbon bolsters one's morale. My last drink was taking hold, and at that moment I actually believed I could ride. I made a dash at Killjoy, caught blindly at the saddle, got my foot into the stirrup, and swung myself up.

Unfortunately the foot I got into the stirrup was the right one—and

the wrong one. As a result, when I landed in the saddle I found I was up the wrong way, and was facing the rump of the animal.

There was nothing I could do about it. I couldn't turn round without being bounced off, and the way the animal was bucking the only way I could get off was to fall off. This I was loth to do.

I maintained a vice-like grip on the rear of the saddle and waited for the groom to quiet the horse. It seemed to me that I waited quite a long time. The amusement of the assembly grew with every bounce I suffered.

I finally got fed up at being the butt of their laughter. 'All right, all right,' I called in all directions (literally, for one minute I was facing one way, and the next the horse had pranced round in another). 'I bet I can ride this horse to the Burgoynes' backwards.' I did not know the Burgoynes, and was only waiting for a chance to slip off my steed, but I just had to say something.

'Twenty bucks,' a voice called. Its owner may, of course, have just been counting the number of times I had been thrown in the air.

'I'll make it thirty,' called out George.

'All right,' I said, without thinking farther ahead than my words.

It was at this point that the groom let go. I have always had a sneaking suspicion that George signalled him to do so, for though he has not much sense of humour he is a great practical joker.

Killjoy wasted not a moment. He bolted. I watched the astonished company receding swiftly from view. Except for the switchback motion it was rather like riding on the observation platform of a train.

I was much too busy to be ashamed of my predicament. Shame, I realized, would come later. Now, it was all I could do to hold on.

Straight down the drive shot Killjoy, and out into the road. He hesitated for an instant. Then, making up his mind where he wanted to go, he zoomed off to the right.

I doubt whether any of you have the slightest idea how difficult it is to control a runaway horse while riding backwards on him. There is just nothing one can grip hold of that will in any way convey the idea to the animal that you want him to stop. In my extremity I even tried grabbing hold of his extremity. Perhaps fortunately, I was unable to grip his tail properly and my efforts came so near to unseating me that I desisted.

The road we were galloping down was a dirt country road which ran towards Centerville and joined the main hard-surface highway on the outskirts of the town. If only the horse would turn left when we got

I   [125]

to the main road we should be headed out into the country again, and
there was some hope that he might tire of his wild career. If he turned
right I hated to think what would happen.

He turned right.

We flashed into the town in high, and then occurred a series of
happenings that made me realize that the horse's conduct was not due to
hysteria, nervous tension, or even psychotic tendencies, but was entirely
dictated by the fact that he was a nasty-minded practical joker like his
master. As soon as we got properly into the town he slowed down to a
fast trot. I attempted to take advantage of his slackening pace to turn
round, but every time I tried he gave a buck that pointed out quite clearly
to me that he would not tolerate any such action. I therefore resigned
myself to trotting backwards through Centerville at the hour when the
good people of the town were just leaving church and returning home to
their Sunday dinners.

Such is the unquenchable spirit of man that in spite of being *abductus
ad absurdum* I attempted to invest my passage with some threads of dignity.
I figured that if I appeared to be enjoying myself people might think I was
actually riding backwards on purpose, for some good reason of my own.
I therefore bowed and waved to the crowds of people who were making
their way homewards along the street. I was pleased to observe that I
received a number of friendly grins and waves back.

'The Yanks are coming!' I yelled cheerfully, shielding my eyes with
my hand as I pretended to peer back along the way I had come.

I didn't stick around long enough, as you might say, to observe
closely the results of my little gambit, but I did see a number of people
running into the middle of the road and looking in the direction in which
I was pointing. It struck me at the time that they were making much ado
about nothing. I figured they couldn't be taking me seriously. Nowadays,
far from being a cause for alarm, the advent of the Yanks in the South
is the signal for Southerners joyously to hang out signs saying, 'Real
Southern cooking', or 'Genuine Confederate Cannonballs, one dollar
each'—two equally unpalatable commodities which they seem to think
the Northerners are after.

At a later date a friend sent me a clipping from the *Centerville Clarion*
about a stranger who, on a Sabbath morn, rode through the town crying
'The tanks are coming!' It appeared that for some time after I had left
the townspeople were hanging around hoping to see the passing of a

U.S. armoured corps. I don't know who they thought I was, unless perhaps it was the Commandant who was both keeping an eye on his troops and clearing the way for them at the same time.

The second incident which made me realize that Killjoy was acting in accordance with a deep-laid plot between him and George occurred in the centre of the town, where there is the only set of traffic-lights Centerville possesses.

These lights were red when we arrived there, and there were a half-dozen cars waiting for them to change. Killjoy stopped dead, right behind one of the last of these cars, and next to a large open sports-type car with Ohio licence plates. In this car were a paunchy man with angry, bloodshot eyes, whose scalp looked as if it had melted in the heat and had slipped down around his ears, and an angular lady with a mouth like a bear trap. They were, I concluded, obviously husband and wife, or they wouldn't have put up with each other for a minute. They wore the antagonistic look of those who suspect all comers of not being 100 per cent like themselves. In my case their suspicions were well founded, for in my present predicament I was far removed from anything approaching their standards of acceptability.

The shock of sudden cessation of movement almost caused me to fall off. I decided that now was my chance to part from Killjoy. As soon as the horse felt me move on his back, however, he started to buck. I fastened myself like a leech to the saddle again, whereupon he quieted down. I tried to get off once more, with the same result. I gave it up. Wearily I decided that the only thing to do was to wait until this grue-some animal got out of the traffic and then to jump off, even if it meant a few bruises or worse.

The lights seemed to take for ever changing. I thought they must have gotten stuck, but I saw they were operated by a policeman in a box who was busy giving directions to somebody. After a while I began to get restive under the unwinking stares of the man and woman in the car. I decided that something had to be done to ease the situation socially.

'Nice day,' I remarked casually.

The man regarded me with profound distaste and said nothing. His wife, however, could not contain her curiosity. 'Do you always ride like that?' she grated.

'Like what?' I said with sang-froid.

'Backwards!'

[127]

'Excuse me, ma'am,' I said in my best Southern-fried drawl, 'I ain't.'

This shook her husband out of his silence. 'What do you mean?' he bellowed. 'Anyone can see you're back to front.'

'No, sir,' I replied with a slightly alcoholic grin, for the Bourbon was kicking around inside me, 'I ain't. It's the horse that is.'

He went a sort of purple colour. Just then the lights turned green and the cars ahead started to move. Killjoy followed suit.

' 'Bye,' I called back to them as they sat in stunned inaction in the car. 'Follow me and I'll tell you where you've been.'

They did not take my advice and I saw them in the distance making a somewhat shaky left-hand turn.

Once out of town the horse resumed speed, and I was hard put to it to stay on, even though he was no longer galloping flat out. I waited, hoping for a nice bit of bank on to which I might tumble.

About half a mile up the road Killjoy suddenly turned off the main highway and I found that we were rushing up what appeared to be a private driveway. I screwed my head round and saw in front of us a large rambling frame house. There was a white-fenced pasture next to it with some horses in it, and some people were sitting in deck-chairs on the front lawn with iced glasses in their hands. I figured that if they were not at that moment talking about riding they soon would be.

Killjoy rode straight up to the fence and stopped dead. A mare detached herself from the group of horses in the field and trotted over to him. They were whispering sweet nuzzlings into each other's ears when I slipped quickly to the ground.

Once there I became afflicted with the sort of vertigo that attacks people on land after a long and rough sea voyage. I staggered towards the party on the lawn hoping they would not think me intoxicated.

A tall, elderly gentleman in a white suit and white goatee got up and came towards me. He wore a thin black ribbon instead of a necktie and looked like an advertisement for Genuine Kentucky Bourbon, or Real Southern Hospitality.

I thought my best approach would be the light one. If I could explain jocularly that I had just been riding backwards for a wager, I might escape with no further traumas to my psyche. I was really not feeling at all bad. Killjoy apparently had shaken all the Bourbon to the top of my head, for I had a pleasant sensation of not quite being on the ground. This struck me as being just as well, for the ground was still heaving.

I felt I had an explanation to make to the gentleman on whose property I was trespassing. I smiled genially at him and held out my hand.

'Howdy, pardner,' I said. 'I've just brought the good news from Aix to Ghent.'

His blue eyes twinkled and his goatee quivered as he grinned. 'You got it backwards, son,' he said.

'That's all right, Cunnel,' I replied blithely. 'I brought it backwards.'

He laughed. 'If it ain't bein' too inquisitive,' he said, 'what are you settin' out to prove?'

'Nothing particular,' I said. 'I've just been riding around.'

He gave me a sharp look. 'What style of ridin' do you call that? Chinese? They tell me that they write backwards.'

I laughed with carefree abandon. 'I was just letting the horse have its head. I took its tail.'

'More comfortable thataway?' he suggested.

'It was a toss-up,' I giggled. 'He tossed me. Heads I tail, tails I tail. As a matter of fact I did it on a bet.'

He took my arm. 'Ah think you'd better come and sit down, son,' he said. 'T'ain't good to be standin' around in this hot sun. You get so that you cain't think straight after a while.'

'Thank you,' I said. 'I'd like to, but first I'd better see to my horse. You haven't got a shotgun handy, have you?'

He regarded me with astonishment. 'T'ain't no time of day to go huntin',' he said. 'Besides, what could you shoot?'

'Horses,' said I, making a ploy with an old joke.

He looked over to where Killjoy was munching the grass. 'What makes you so down on him?' he asked. 'He looks a quiet enough animal. Say, wait a minute, haven't Ah seen him before somewhere?'

'You could have,' I said, 'but if I were you I should'nt try to presume on your acquaintance. He's the meanest thing since Simon Legree.'

'He looks mighty familiar,' he said. 'I've got it. That's George Dexter's horse. He's got a girl-friend over heah and he's broken loose once or twice before and come over to see her.'

'Has he now!' I exclaimed. I was intrigued by this sidelight on George's character.

'Yes,' said the Colonel. 'That's her over theah.' He pointed to the mare with Killjoy.

Regretfully I readjusted my ideas. 'Would you mind if I left him here and hitch-hiked back to the Dexters'?' I asked. 'I don't much relish the thought of having anything more to do with that overgrown coyote.'

'No, suh!' he cried. 'We'll look after him till George sends for him. I'll drive you home mahself. But come and have a drink first. Burgoyne's mah name. What's yours?'

I did a double take. 'What did you say your name was?' I gasped.

'Burgoyne. General Lucifer B. Burgoyne. Folks mostly just call me General, but Lucy's mah nickname. Ah don't mind. It's what they called me at West Point.'

'General,' I crowed, doing a joyful hornpipe in front of him, 'you're a sight for sore eyes and a sore something else, if you take my meaning. You just won me thirty dollars.'

He did not seem surprised or even interested. 'That's all right, son,' he said. 'Always glad to do something for a friend of George's. His father and I were born and raised in the same town and were business associates for many years.'

I was staggered. 'But George is a New Yorker!' I cried.

'Yes suh, yes indeedy!' he replied. 'His folks and mine both came from Dutchess County. An ancestor of mine was kin to the British General, but he was in the boat with Washington when he crossed the Delaware.'

It sure doesn't do to take anything for granted down South nowadays, for the South ain't what she used to be—no, sir, not by a long way!

I was well into my third Bourbon when George and his friends arrived. I greeted their astonished looks benignly.

'You shertainly took your time,' I remarked. 'Gen'l Lucy and I were wond'ring what had happened to you.'

George's face was a study in purple. 'Where's Killjoy?' he choked.

I waved an airy hand towards the field where my mount was playfully biting his girl-friend's ear. 'A nice horse,' I said. 'But frankly, George, he lacks spirit.'

'You mean you *rode* him here?' George gasped.

I swayed forward and put my hand in a friendly fashion on his shoulder. 'I sure did, you schemin' old houn' dawg,' I crowed genially. 'And backwards all the way! In the words of that immortal horseman, Julius Caesar, "I conquered, I saw, and I came". And now, pal, how's about those thirty bucks?'

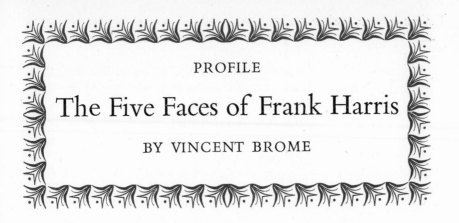

PROFILE

The Five Faces of Frank Harris

BY VINCENT BROME

I F YOU met Frank Harris in the flesh there was nothing you could do about it. He *imposed* himself on whoever encountered him. No matter whether it was Lord Francis Williams, a close friend of Queen Victoria, Oscar Wilde, or the toughest journalist of the day, he quickly made an overwhelming impression. His stocky, barrel-chested person, clothed in carefully tailored suits and ornate waitcoasts, was striking. His carefully cultivated moustaches, swinging twelve inches apart, added fierceness to his swarthy countenance. The heels of his shoes, built up an extra two inches to compensate for his mere five feet five inches, gave him an odd, stilted stance. Taken together, his spats, gold watch-chain, ornate waistcoats, and moustaches produced on the observer something of the effect of the old-fashioned cinema villain. There was about the total impression, a flashiness, and not even the panache with which Frank Harris entered distinguished company, or the cascade of poetry he could quote on the slightest provocation, quite obliterated the traces of—was it the rogue in his countenance?

Come back for a moment to the year 1896, to a spring day in that year, with Piccadilly thronged by crowds and a rubber-tyred hansom threading its way through the horse traffic. The knob of a beautiful cane knocks imperiously on the window and a mangy horse draws to a stand-still, approximately opposite the Café Royal. Throwing twice his fare to the driver with the air of an aristocrat distributing largesse, Frank Harris stalks into the Café Royal, to be greeted by a crowd of people ranging from shady business promoters to distinguished authors. All appear to be in a state of some consternation. Fifty guests were milling around the Café Royal that day, summoned to a great luncheon party by telegrams, only to find that Frank Harris, their host, had forgotten to book a table.

[131]

'No table!' Harris roared when he heard the news. 'No table!' and the repeated words echoed thunderously in the hush of the Café Royal. 'Then they must make one!' The manager came hurrying up, and Frank's voice, deep as a Russian choir, was heard ordering a table to be inserted down the centre of the salon. He clearly expected this impossible feat to be carried out in ten minutes. He was the Great Frank Harris, and luncheon tables of any required proportion sprang up at his bidding, restaurant managers brushing aside lesser mortals to meet his requirements. The manager on this occasion did not disappoint him.

At the cost of considerable disruption a number of trestle tables were joined together down the centre of the room, the guests took their places, and soup was followed by fish, and fish by great haunches of venison. Suddenly Harris's voice broke out above the hubbub. 'Homosexuality?' it said. 'No. I know nothing of the joys of homosexuality. My friend Oscar Wilde can no doubt tell you all about that.'

In the embalmed correctness of Victorian England such words were volcanic, and a hush ran down the table, everyone looking askance at Harris. As if quite oblivious of the shock he had caused, Harris suddenly continued, in a voice which echoed right round the restaurant: 'But I must say that if Shakespeare had asked me I should have had to submit.'

Extraordinarily, the man who could be mistaken for a circus proprietor or travelling salesman had a habit of confusing himself with two unexpected figures—Shakespeare and Christ—and he would say, with deadly seriousness, to a horrified Oxford don: 'I suppose Christ goes deeper than I do, but I have a wider experience.' There was an even more interesting moment when Harris began a sentence to the self-same don with the words: 'Let me come to those things in Shakespeare I couldn't have written myself. . . .'

Happily free from anything so depressing as modesty, he boomed and browbeat his way through the 'nineties, silencing his critics with a brassy lion's roar and a flood of Irish eloquence. He looked astonished at anyone who did not understand that his kind of genius was subject to laws quite different from the normal. He spoke of cosmic morals replacing human; he spoke of lords of the intellect dominating the earth. 'I would rather have a third-class ticket round my own brain than a first-class ticket round the world,' he told Oscar Wilde, and tended to challenge Oscar's appearance with his own perfectly knotted Eton tie, Queensberry waistcoat, diamond tie stud, gold cuff-links, and waxed moustaches. But the

picture which emerges from his contemporaries of a thick-set bull of a man thrusting his way ruthlessly to success with women, editors, and money, needs closer examination.

There were, in fact, five Frank Harrises. First came the man of action who could dominate fifty guests at the Café Royal, whose voice reached two tones lower than the ordinary scale, and who once rode the American range as a cowboy rustler. In later years it was difficult to visualize the elegant, top-hatted, swarthy roué transformed into a cowboy with high-heeled boots, 'chaps', and a flannel shirt, riding out on a burning hot day through the dusty streets of Kansas City. But that was what happened to Frank Harris in his teens. For nearly a year he rode the range in a manner calculated to make very good reading later in life. The torture which he endured in the saddle, before he learned to 'fry' his hips in salt water and whisky every night, was commonplace to every cowboy. The discovery that innocent-looking bronchos could perform manœuvres unknown to nature while onlookers grunted with expressionless faces—'Quiet to ride, ain't she?'—was equally a cliché from any Western film.

In the confusion of truth and lies surrounding Harris's cowboy life the worst doubts might have dissolved if he had not insisted on exaggerating every incident out of all recognition. But the strange mathematics of truth left a considerable core of hard fact if one divided his lies by two—or should it be three? Certainly, one moonless night he stole 2,000 head of cattle from a wealthy hacienda in Mexico, and shot down a man who tried to intervene; certainly he met and argued with the legendary Bill Hickok, learnt to break-in horses, fought a number of Mexicans, and became familiar with the yellow-eyed beauties who smelt at a distance of some yards and were liable to leave more than memories of passion among their customers. The splendid crown to these adventures came with a midnight dash through encircling Indians and a desperate one-hour's race on foot, when his horse Shiloh collapsed and Harris soared across rough country with indelible purpose, holding to the stirrup leather of his buddy Reece. The supreme irony of bringing U.S. State Troopers to the aid of cattle rustlers did not seem to occur to Harris. The smell of cattle, leather, woodsmoke, raw beef, and sometimes blood remained romantic in his memory. But Harris, the man of action, was a romantic in so many ways. He also possessed far too good an intelligence to stand the cowboy's life for long.

Returning to London, a young man of twenty-six, with no special

training, no friends, and fewer prospects, within eighteen months he had taken over the editorship of a big London paper. Within two and a half years he was the talk of London. The tough, brandy-bitten ex-cow-puncher pushed his way ruthlessly to the top ranks of journalism. He later explained the principles which drove him. 'I edited the *Evening News* first as a scholar and man of the world of twenty-eight; nobody wanted my opinions, but as I went downwards and began to edit as I felt at twenty, then at eighteen, then at sixteen, I was more successful; but when I got to my tastes at fourteen years of age I found instantaneous response. Kissing and fighting were the only things I cared for at thirteen or fourteen, and these are the things the English public desires and enjoys today.'

It was in the dark, ancient offices of the *Evening News* that the struggle began between the man of action from the American plains, liable to knock down one of his staff in a burst of rage, and the Great Editor, trying to disguise the cowboy under a new sophistication. The man of action drove up the circulation of the *News* from 7,000 to 70,000 by the simple expedient of revolutionizing the character of the news stories until the once staid and very Conservative evening paper carried headlines like: 'Assault on an Austrian Girl'—'Extraordinary Charge Against a Clergyman'—'Gross Outrage on a Female'.

The man of action arrived in the dim old offices at eight in the morning and set the staff quaking as they had never quaked before. Sitting under a gas lamp at a scarred wooden desk he bellowed 'Boy!' in a voice like thunder—or 'Jones!'—for the Chief Reporter, and he would literally hiss into the mouthpiece by which he communicated with lesser denizens in the rooms below, when he did not try to make his voice heard by simply raising it to its full pitch.

But the Great Editor kept muttering in the background, the man who understood the meaning of style and originality in writing continuously rebelled against the slip-shod stuff which passed for writing in his news reports. Sheer opportunism had driven him into a false sympathy with the appetites of the masses who could increase the circulation of the *Evening News*, but the serious editor in him despised the readers he served. Slowly, the necessity to increase circulation was inhibited by the desire to make himself acceptable in the highest Tory circles, and the struggle between two sides of his nature intensified.

The last burst of sensational journalism brought him low spectacularly.

He printed intimate details from a divorce case, convinced that prurience was the third great factor calculated to increase circulation, and the authorities indicted him for obscene libel. In those mid-Victorian days one could exploit sweated labour with some pretence to serving the community, sit, with immense dignity, on the board of a fraudulent company, and even become a highly respected member of the House of Commons by electoral deception, but to be brought before the law courts for printing obscenities—this was too much. The directors of the *Evening News* decided that Harris must go.

Paradoxically, the second Frank Harris—the Great Editor—came into his own on the death of the editor of the *Evening News*. First he took over the editorship of the *Fortnightly*, that far more sober-sided organ of public opinion where the mandarins of the day wrote about very correct matters in pompous English. Then he moved to the *Saturday Review* and edited the paper to the top of his bent, completely transforming it. The old staff were sent packing in a manner which H. G. Wells never forgot. He arrived at the office one day to find people ascending and descending the stairs, some in a bull-rush of rage, and the 'roar of a remembered voice told me that Harris was on the higher level . . . having a glorious time of it. . . . He had summoned most of the former staff to his presence in order to read out scraps from their contributions . . . and to demand in the presence of his Dear Gahd and his faithful henchman Silk, why the hell they wrote like that? It was a Revolution—the twilight of the Academic.'

In the early issues, under Harris's editorship, H. G. Wells wrote enthusiastically about a novelist called Joseph Conrad, whose book, *Almayer's Folly*, struck a strange new note in English literature; George Bernard Shaw savaged Shakespeare in a manner most unbecoming to the Victorian mind and praised an upstart called Ibsen; Cunninghame Graham wrote vivid travel sketches, and Max Beerbohm satirized whatever took his fancy. Six names destined to become literary bywords were launched into literature by Frank Harris the Editor.

It was at this point that the third Frank Harris suddenly burst the banks of the other two and momentarily dominated everything. The sensualist in Harris was deliberately cultivated and given every encouragement which a highly erotic imagination could devise. He referred to himself as 'a rattlesnake striking at everything that moves, even the blades of grass'. A man who made a cult of acquiring new mistresses and

became notorious in the end for writing *My Life and Loves*, he could cynically seduce a number of young women, fall in love with one of them, become quite sentimental about female beauty, and deliberately introduce a girl of twelve to highly sophisticated sexual habits, all within six months. His toughness produced, in reaction, sentimentality, and his promiscuity left him unsatisfied. Harris the lover had a habit of shocking people with sexual details of outrageous frankness. He would reveal the intimate habits of prostitutes to a young girl at one of his wife's parties; he was quite capable of suddenly announcing to two impeccably correct middle-class ladies: 'Rape? Any sensible woman would relax and enjoy it.'

It is platitudinous to remark that the third Harris—the Great Lover—had phenomenal virility, and there were clearly many other sides to his nature which rendered women highly susceptible to him. His voice—'like a rustle of iron leaves'—'as if something very profound had spoken to you out of the forest'—could hypnotize girls far younger than he was, but he added something beyond virility, voice, and eloquence to his love-making. As one mistress who loved him wrote: 'He always talked as if he held the key to life—with a big "L". As if only with his help could one pass into the kingdom of experience. What nonsense that all was about Passion and Freedom! And how it impressed one! And one was sorry for him, too. . . . One thought of him as a rebel who had refused success in disgust at the price one has to pay for it. Yet there *was* something there—a tangled, troubled light. Disturbed, I know, betrayed, sullied, but there! . . . I still see the horizon of his eyes and talk flaming like a sunset. . . . And yet it's gone—how it's gone. I suppose because it was all so unreal. I thought it real enough then—but there was too much "Love" and too little natural affection. And yet . . . there was something beautiful there once, even if it had died. . . .'

There remained the woman in Hugh Kingsmill's biography who said: 'He hasn't the least idea how to touch a woman's heart, her intellect, or her passion. He is brute but not brute enough, or not brute in the way that every woman of flesh and blood will forgive—and more than forgive.'

Harris plunged into his torrent of sensuality with considerable glee. Justification for his conduct varied with his mood and frequently he was brutally honest about his enjoyment of simple lust, an experience not unknown, he claimed, to every man alive. Plunge as he did into animal

indulgences, with little regard for the consequences, there were times when he paused breathless before the beauty of a lovely body. As the names accumulated—Mary, Frances, Christine, Pamela—one person remained constant, Nellie, his wife. If this pale-skinned, auburn-haired, wide-eyed beauty from Ireland showed the ravages of the ordeal to which she had committed herself—marriage to Frank Harris—there were long periods when he respected her. She herself was a fascinating mixture, capable of behaving like a perfect lady, remaining a silent and decorative presence amongst the Niagara of talk common to so many of Frank's friends, and sometimes, when the guests had gone, raising her voice to fishwife pitch and blistering Frank for some small neglect.

In the rich web of his love-life one other strand remained constant. Dramatically casting himself in the role of the noble rebel, sacrificing his talents to put society right, he brilliantly exploited equivalent characteristics in every other young woman he met. A combination of the young virgin and the born *revoltée* was irresistible to him. Playing skilfully on every rebellious note, he attacked just those targets which young women despised, and in no time had them saying: 'That's true—oh, how true.' When they finally became his mistresses, almost without exception they did so with the air of giving themselves to the cause of a Great Artist who was breathing a new, clean spirit into the cobwebbed places of life.

An American student of twenty faithfully fulfilled this ritual one week-end, and involved Harris in serious trouble. Ostensibly discussing literature with H. L. Mencken, Harris returned from 'an abandoned forty-eight hours' with the American student to find his wife waiting for him at the station in New York. She was coldly furious. In the taxi he tried to put his arm round her and she pushed him away, turned, and spat at him: 'Understand clearly—either that little bitch goes or I do.'

Suddenly Frank lost his temper. They launched terrific tirades on each other and fought like hell-cats until the taximan looked fearfully over his shoulder, afraid that murder might be committed in his taxi. That night Nellie said she had had enough. She stormed about the house packing her bags . . . but in the morning she was still there.

In the middle years, as the different incarnations of Harris took shape, he always underwent a period of great irritability, and it was even possible to witness the ferment on his face as the editor gave place to the lover or the lover the scoundrel. It was like a man struggling out of one skin into another; but as he grew older he became a much more

skilled chameleon, rapidly summoning the lover, editor, blackmailer, writer, or scoundrel as the situation required. Whenever a desired end seemed within reach of one of his five personalities he swiftly swept away the other four. That was the main purpose of the exercise; to bring alive the person who could win the desired reward in the shortest possible time. Half his success lay in his skill as an actor, and it was a considerable experience to watch the editor slowly diminish and give place to the scoundrel, the first a man who could quote huge passages in an organ-voice from half the literature of Western Europe, the second . . . well . . .

The scoundrel was the fourth face of Frank Harris, a face which first settled into place in the early nineteen-hundreds, when his two extravagant hotel ventures in the South of France threatened to ruin him. Still vigorous, thrusting, upright, a hint of duplicity was evident in the swarthy countenance of the scoundrel. His ears were big and ugly, his hair coming down over a beetling brow gave him an almost Neanderthal appearance, his moustaches bristled across their twelve inches, and his waistcoats were even more ornate. This Harris would come striding into the office of some city business man, his homburg hat set at a rakish angle, his spats spotlessly white, his cuffs shot out the correct three inches, and plough his way through any outer defences, scattering lesser staff in confusion. Tapping his gold-nobbed stick on whatever object—human or otherwise—offered itself, he then announced that he had AN APPOINTMENT. No exaggeration of print could convey the mighty assurance he put into that single sentence.

The result of the appointment might be a business deal in which Harris talked loftily about business honesty only to collapse, with considerable skill, into expediency and worse. His first direct plunge into the dark waters of Horatio Bottomley came when he persuaded Lord Alfred Douglas to invest several thousand pounds in the Cesari Reserve, an investment guaranteed, he said, to make money. He did not in fact sell Douglas the stock at all. He simply transferred certificates of the same value from holdings of his own in the land on which the Reserve was built. In effect he 'unloaded the stock' and legally the £3,000 became Harris's property. On the principle that Lords in the same family should be equally easy to bamboozle, he next sold the brother of Lord Alfred Douglas shares said to belong to the Rich Man's Reserve, which really covered another and doomed property, the Palace of Monte Carlo.

Discovering a natural taste for this kind of thing, Harris quickly

graduated through one fraud after another until he challenged Horatio Bottomley himself. He was passing Bottomley's house one day when he observed, leaving it with some stealth, a famous man who had lately come under scathing attack in Bottomley's paper *John Bull*. Harris immediately knocked on the door, was shown into Bottomley's study, and said: 'Give me £500 of the hush money that man has just paid you and I won't say a word about it.'

Bottomley glowered at Harris, hesitated for a long moment, and then went to his safe and counted out the £500. Stuffing the bunch of notes into his pocket in silence, Harris walked to the door and opened it as Bottomley said: 'How did you know?'

'I didn't,' Harris said, and closed the door behind him.

In the middle years Harris the writer, Harris the lover, and Harris the editor struggled furiously to keep Harris the scoundrel in his proper place, but as advancing years brought greater hardship, the cunning *alter ego* fought his way to the top with increasing power and frequency. Presently, a positive malignancy distinguished some of the scoundrel's activities. An American, Buckland Plummer, claimed that Harris made over sixty thousand dollars by a system of fraudulent begging letters, and highly dramatic hints of some form of white slavery came from the same source. However, one difficulty constantly arose. Whatever new conspiracy the scoundrel launched into, time and again he had to turn to the writer for help, and inevitably he did it with very bad grace. It needed all Harris's considerable powers of writing to give the begging letters of the scoundrel their full persuasive subtlety. Bogus prospectuses written by the writer rang with such eloquence and conviction that scores of innocent investors were duped. The scoundrel despised the writer but could not do without him.

It was this fifth Frank Harris, the writer, who continually struggled to assert himself against the worst that the other Harrises could do. Pushed down, duped, and deceived, the sprite which insisted that words were beautiful things, and literature a high calling, did succeed in making his voice heard among the rush and clangour of Harris's brassier selves. This was the person who could be deeply moved by events which would have aroused ribald comments in the scoundrel. This was the person who once so vividly evoked the enchantment of London. 'London to me is like a woman with wet, draggled, dirty skirts (it's always raining in London), and at first you turn from her in disgust, but soon you discover

[139]

that she has glorious eyes lighting up her pale wet face. . . . And if you admire her eyes and tell her so passionately one mid-summer evening, when the sunshine is a golden mist, she will give you her lips and take you to her heart, and you will find in her spirit, depths undreamed of, passionate devotions, smiling self-sacrifices, and loving gentle tendance till your eyes dim at the sweet memory of her. And ever afterwards you, the alien and outcast and pariah of this all-hating world, will have a soft heart for London. You will find magic and mystery in her fogs, as Whistler did, and in her gardens some June morning you will wake to find her temperate warmth of desire more enchanting than any tropic heat. . . .'

Harris the writer not merely wrote some beautiful descriptive passages; he produced a few very fine short stories which pleased no less an eye than Arnold Bennett's. Nor did it by any means stop there. Harris wrote over twenty books and two plays, and if the majority of these were second- and third-rate, his book on Shakespeare fell into a different category and his biographies of Wilde and Bernard Shaw make supremely good reading today.

There, then, were the five Frank Harrises. Now the writer on the crest of a sudden inspiration dominated the scene, now the demands of the lover overwhelmed the necessity to launch a new book, and then the blackmailer was liable to rear up as he suddenly saw a chance of outwitting all the other selves.

And yet something is missing; something essential to the kernel of Frank Harris is very much missing in all this; because the brandy-bitten tycoon who might ruthlessly exploit an old friend had known another and quite different range of experience. He had known what it meant to be hopelessly and romantically in love, he sometimes told the truth about himself when other people would have lied; the savage censure which his conduct brought down on his head he accepted and overcame with great courage; he cared very much about literature and he cherished somewhere inside himself a pool of sensitivity with considerable tragic awareness. It broke through in his own last words: 'There is an end of time and an end of the evil thereof; when delight is gone out of thee and desire is dead, thy mourning shall not be for long. . . . Yet the adventure of life was glorious and the magic of moments of love and pity and understanding beyond description or thanks.'

[140]

ITALIAN TOURS

VENICE

in photographs by Barbara Gomperts

DANTIS·POETAE·SEPVLCRVM

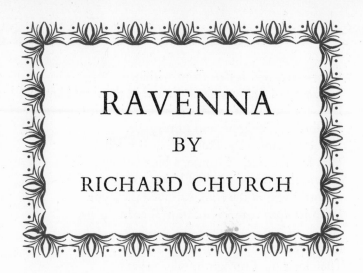

RAVENNA

BY

RICHARD CHURCH

HERE in the sad city, the city burdened
With time, and the old enmity of salt,
Man's possessive mother from whose womb,
Weltering ocean, gradually he was born,
I stand in a reminiscent day of October
The heavy month, the month of memories.

Ravenna! Shape the name with your inward mouth,
With loud, interpretive silence, recalling
The slow procession, broken dynasties,
The rocklike Empire shattered and reformed
In minor jewels that refract the light,
Italy, France, Britain, splinters chipped
From Rome, and facetted by Gothic hands
To flash again the gleam of civic life.

It started in Ravenna, after the fall
Of Rome, and all Rome spelled; the law,
The unity, the Ciceronian rhythm,
The sweet sophistication of Catullus;
Horace, the shrewd master of restraint;
Virgil, given to golden numbers in a world
Seemingly poised for ever upon peace.

[159]

Over-sweet and rotten from within,
That way of life was plucked, and in the thumbing
Bruised: but still it assuaged the Gothic thirst,
Soothed the Visigoth and Ostrogoth,
And even tamed the Hun. What was left
Was but the rind of Rome, a blood-stained rind
Where slavering fangs had bitten too deep of the fruit.
And still within the rind, survived the stone
With its deep core, civilization's seed.

It was planted in Ravenna by the Goth,
Theodoric the Ostrogoth, who valued
What he had raped. He sleeps there now,
His mausoleum massive, slowly sinking
As all the ancient city is slowly sinking,
Too heavy with history for its foundations
In the delta mud. He lies outside the city,
This Arian, as single as his God,
Rejected by the Holy Trinity
Whose images still glitter in the domes
Of Saints Vitale and Apollinare,
Rich from the murex and new-minted gold.

They were riches enough: but another mosaic
Out-glitters even those; the words which Dante
Polished and patterned, closing the crown in Ravenna,
Achieving in his exile—Paradise!

World-conqueror, world-poet lie asleep,
Fellows in power in a foundering city.
Tread reverently there. Go to Ravenna
To look on infamy, to look on fame.
Beneath the campaniles and the domes
The delta slowly breathes—slowly breathes.
Tread quietly, for fear that sleeper wakes.

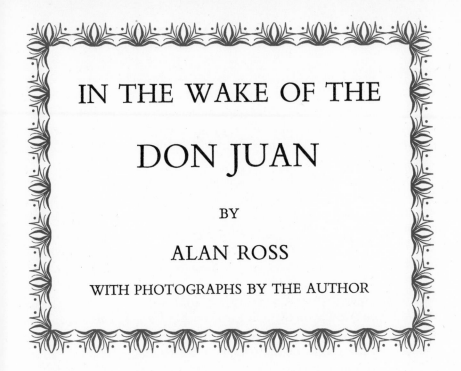

IN THE WAKE OF THE

DON JUAN

BY

ALAN ROSS

WITH PHOTOGRAPHS BY THE AUTHOR

THE Golfo dei Poeti it is called, that blue double bay, shaped like a sea-horse, which has at its mouth Porto Venere, and at its tail Lerici. No one can sail it now without being aware, at each swing of the helm, of Shelley's *Don Juan* and its little *Sandolino*, of Byron's impeccable *Bolivar*, cruising these off-shore waters, from the Cinque Terre down past the marble quarries of Carrara to Livorno, point of departure, on that fatal stormy night of July 8th, 1822, for Shelley, Williams, and Charles Vivian on their mysterious last journey.

Yet if it is in terms of Shelley first, and then Byron, that we in turn, as summer rusts its way into autumn, patrol the coast, there are echoes, too, of another English poet, D. H. Lawrence, whom we have followed down from Garda, and who, comfortably installed at Fiascherino, a mile or so down the coast from Lerici, spent most of an unusually contented year. 'When one walks,' wrote Lawrence, who came here from Switzerland on foot, 'one must travel west or south. If one turns northward or eastward it is like walking down a cul-de-sac, to the blind end. So it has been since the Crusaders came home satiated, and the Renaissance saw the Western sky as an archway into the future.'

Let us then follow the coast, known more prosaically as the Spezia Riviera, from north to south, and, disregarding our usual base at Lerici, work our way down from Monterosso at the far end of the Cinque Terre to Via Reggio, itself within easy driving distance of Pisa and the two palazzi marked today with the plaques of Lord Byron and Percy Bysshe Shelley.

The Italy of English poets is scarcely less complete than it is of the great Latin and Italian, but nowhere, except perhaps in Venice, do you get so persistent a feeling of their physical presence as when, sliding into the smoother waters between the island of Palmaria and Porto Venere, you get your first glimpse of San Terenzo, with the white powdery arches of Shelley's Casa Magni catching the eye from far across the bay.

But that is not yet, for supposing, having slipped out at first light from the cradling harbour at Portofino, we were to nose close inshore by the beetling traffic on the hills through Rapallo and Sestri Levante, it would be Monterosso that found us at noon, the white boat rocking at anchor, the sheer cliffs of the Cinque Terre blinding out of a colour-less sky, and along the beach the rust-coloured nets spread like drying stockings.

The Cinque Terre—Monterosso, Vernazza, Corniglia, Manarola, Riomaggiore, the names of the first villages, reachable as yet by no motor road, roll off the tongue as richly as does the wine for which this region, since the time of Petrarch, has been justly praised: '*indi al benigno sole—spiegano i vigneti delizia a Bacco—e Monterosso e i gioghi di Corniglia—famosa cui Natura diede meglio—al mellifluo licor—che di Falerno—ai colli lodati e a Meroe antica*'—so Petrarch describes it in *De Africa*, and Flavio Biondo, a hundred years later, in the mid-fifteenth century, corroborated it: '*quae loca non in Italia magis quam in Galliis Britaniaque sive Anglia a vini odoratissimi suavissimique excellentia sunt celebria*'. 'Smooth and sweet-smelling'; and still in the twentieth century these same wines, though often blended, have a quality to them that is rare in Italy.

These five villages, more or less equidistant from one another, and each quite distinctive in atmosphere, nevertheless share certain characteristics. Firstly, they are built into the rock, squeezed between sea and cliff—westward-facing, marine villages that scratch vines and olives from their dry backbone, and whose only escape is by sea. Some day the motor road will be blasted through the rock, as already has been the tunnel that carries the Rome express; but for the moment the people of the Cinque Terre

MONTEROSSO

SAN TERENZO

LERICI

live from and on the sea, scarcely touched by progress, Vespa-free and serene. Linked only by the narrowest of goat-tracks, the winding Via Dell'Amore, they cultivate their vines and grow their olives on terraces as steep as ladders, with the half-moons of white beaches bracketing their summers together.

Castle ruins, sanctuary, and, most beautiful of all, striped Pisan-romanesque church of the thirteenth century, with splendid façade and rose window dusted by salt spray—these they most of them possess, so that they are perfectly circumscribed, complete within their neat, similar histories. Altars and columns of pink and green Levanto marble turn the much-defaced baroque interiors of these ship-like structures into cool grottoes. The fishing-boats, pink, green, honey-coloured, crowd the narrow beaches, seeming to dissolve like *gelati* in the heat. With antique gestures, fingers to hip and hand to head, a girl sways down the winding street, a jar or washing on her hair. On the sand a big toe twitches the net round which swarthy, crouching figures under straw hats squat mending.

Of these five villages Monterosso, boasting two beaches, is the largest. The pink-washed houses, their balconies bursting with flowers, all but meet over vegetable-and-fruit-blocked alleys: the tough, wiry slope of the hill, sweet with cistus, forms a backdrop to each, and the wavy skeletal lines of vines and olives are smudged here and there by oaks, obscured by the sharp swords of agaves, the rubbery boxing gloves of prickly pear.

We can move again in late afternoon, the sea flush almost to the line of lamp-hung boats, small busy figures bending on the sheer cracked terraces above you. Red head-dresses of the women, like melting sealing-wax, dot the headland, where in spring wallflowers grow down to the rocks and the olives are wreathed by late January in star anemones.

Vernazza next, rockier and steeper still, with the anchovy boats crowding the slipway and the church squatting in matriarchal fashion over the tiny harbour, which only in May, when the fish are at their most plentiful, and again in October for the *vendemmia*, loses its remote and detached air. In winter the houses grip the cliff-top as the waves, from which Monterosso is sheltered by its northern headland, burst over the gunwales of the village. Inside their deep, zig-zagging walls, the shadows of tower and campanile sharpen the air in both winter and summer.

Taking the sunset like a transfer on our sails—saffron, cinnamon, electric green—we skirt Corniglia, harbourless and beachless, houses stamped on to a projecting stump of rock, with only a jetty beneath and a series of swathing terraces keeping it all from falling into the sea, and we tie up for the night in the deep V-shaped harbour of Manarola. Ghika, the Greek painter, has made pictures of his own villages with these severe patterns of wall, rock, terrace, and path, each twisting back in labyrinthine manner, but diagonally always, not curved as here, where in every direction the terraces encircle headlands from rocky summit to foaming hem, and it is the cobbled alleyways themselves, roofs laden with stones and battened down against gales, that thresh around like cornered foxes.

A sea like skimmed milk, next day, for the short run in, past Riomaggiore and the jagged death-dealing Rocce Rosse, to the quiet of Porto Venere and the Golfo dei Poeti.

The Cinque Terre are still much as Shelley and Byron saw them, but from the decks of the *Don Juan*, skimming the Gulf of Spezia, the fishing villages of Porto Venere, San Terenzo, and Lerici, to say nothing of Spezia, must then have looked like small-scale models. Not that the Gulf isn't big enough to contain even greater development; it is; but the remoteness, the sense of isolation, have disappeared.

There are still few more beautiful sights than that which we see as we enter the bay opposite San Terenzo, with Porto Venere and Lerici balanced equally as on scales at either hand. Rounding the narrow run of rock on which the church of S. Pietro dazzles with its black-and-white stripes, it is impossible at first to do more than blot up sensations. The tall thin houses, built against pirates in the twelfth century, throw their rose, grey, and straw reflections on the quayside waters. These houses, one-room wide and as many as eight storeys high, are dominated by a castle whose wall still binds the small community together. The quays all bear stalls, bright with shells and coral and sea-horse brooches, for here the motor road has access, though fortunately not one attached to any of the *autostrade*.

The church of S. Pietro overlooks a swirling grotto, above the entrance of which a plaque pays homage to Byron's physical prowess. Under the heading 'Grotta Byron' it says (in both English and Italian): 'This grotto was the inspiration of Lord Byron. It records the immortal poet who, as a daring swimmer, defied the waves of the sea, from Porto Venere to Lerici.' It is not clear whether this considerable achievement— it must be the best part of five miles across—was ever witnessed, any more than Byron's alleged swimming of the Hellespont; but Trelawney

at least would have had him puking his heart out within shouting distance of Porto Venere.

Opposite Porto Venere lie the rocky islands of Palmaria and Tino, both abandoned defence stations, and now virtually uninhabited except for a small *trattoria* on the former. The stakes of the mussel-beds break the surface in neat formation off the inner shores, and gulls swoop avidly in the wake of the numerous fishing-boats chugging across the Gulf.

Towards San Terenzo now, where the old peeling fishing port is tucked away in the lee of castle and headland, and outside the Casa Magni, now home of the French consul, coloured umbrellas flap in the breeze. From this boat-house, across this sand, Shelley dragged the *Sandolino*, wrapped in his last beguiling dream of romantic happiness with Jane Williams.

> Ariel to Miranda: Take
> This slave of Music, for the sake
> Of him who is the slave of thee.

Even now, wading ashore to examine the inscription above the arches, it is easy to imagine Shelley and Mary, Jane and Edward Williams still inhabiting this gaunt, rather large house, shuttered and solitary, for nothing about it seems to have changed, though Vespas and buses grind and roar beneath its windows. It is a house of great happiness and great sadness, from which the happiness seems to have fled.

Lerici, at the other end of the bay (the sprawling naval front of Spezia is in the other, deeper loop), remains the obvious anchorage, for this is the prettiest small town along the Ligurian coast. Here, too, the port lies in the arm of a castle-heavy headland, the hills behind the pink-and-red harbour-front houses carry their packed oaks and olives sheer to the sky, and an atmosphere of easy compromise is radiated by the sailors, girls, fishermen, and idlers endlessly walking the harbour.

Round this point, between Lerici and Tellaro, the coast grows jagged and deeply indented, thick evergreen scrub curling down over miraculously blue inlets and bays, many of them open only to invaders by sea. Did the *Don Juan* ever heel over into the Conca Azurra, or tack in past the rocks of the Caletta, the bell-tower of Tellaro? Did Lawrence, in his four-roomed pink villa among the olives and vines of Fiascherino, wonder this too? At any rate, he was able to boast in a letter: 'It isn't far from Shelley's San Terenzo—one can see his house across the bay at Lerici—

[169]

but our position is a million times prettier. You have no idea how delightful it is.'

Beyond Tellaro and the cliffs of Monte Marcello the coast swings gently inward before straightening out for the flat pine-fringed burst down to Via Reggio. The Magra river, with its flat-bottomed car ferry, winds down out of the mountains bisecting the sky to the east. Cut into the upper slopes of the hills, with the dust from the marble quarries lying like snow under a true winter snow-line, the fortress villages of Trebbiano and Vezzano look across to the wooded citadel of Ameglia and the sea.

At Bocca di Magra the bathing changes from rock to sand, and now the sailor has only the endless, looping beaches of Forte dei Marmi and Via Reggio between him and the mountains.

Somewhere off these the *Don Juan*, with its death-fixated poet, went to the bottom. On a hot, windless afternoon, the stripes of the beach huts giving a faintly Pisan air to the scene, it all seems a long time ago. It is not here though, nor at Pisa (where only the plaque remains of the Tre Palazzi, where the Shelleys and Williamses had spent their last months just across the Arno from where Byron was installed in the Palazzo Lanfranchi), but in the Golfo dei Poeti, between San Terenzo and Lerici, that the spirits of these two dissimilar English writers, both haunted by Italy and the sea, survive to haunt us too.

GROTTA BYRON, PORTO VENERE

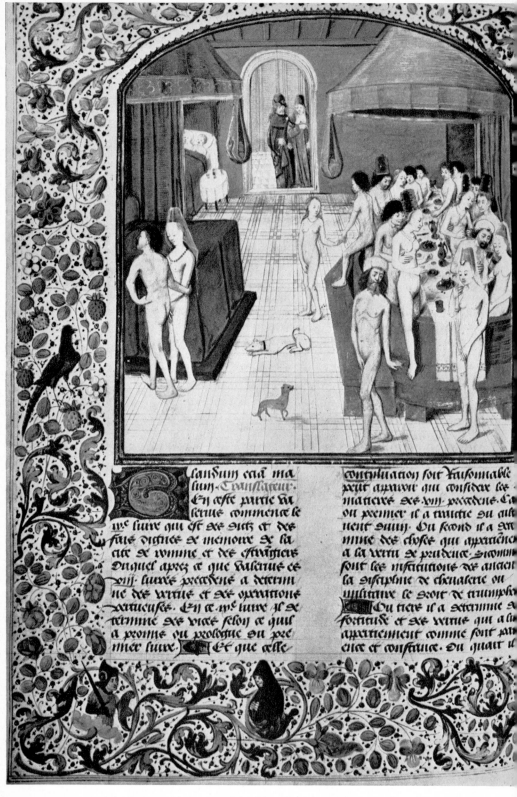

Indulgences of a Parisian dandy, from a picture by Diogenes Tiger, 1824

THE PHILOSOPHY OF THE BATH

BY MARY EDEN

THE PRACTICE of immersing the body in water is almost universal among living things. Life itself originated in water and only emerged from the seas by slow stages. Since those days nearly every animal, including man, makes a periodical re-entry into water for purposes of health, pleasure, or ritual. The earliest form of bathing was practised in the waters of rivers, lakes, and streams, and these are still the bath-houses of primitive peoples today. The aim of immersion in such cases was based on superstition rather than hygiene; washing as an aid to health is not instinctive in the human race, as the fathers and mothers of young children are only too well aware. Water itself was believed to have magical properties,

M   [173]

A Persian bath

and its application to the body was seldom intended simply for the removal of dirt. It was aimed rather at the destruction of evil spirits and, in more advanced communities, at the purification of the soul.

Sir James Frazer tells in *The Golden Bough* how a belief in the magical properties of immersion has persisted into several modern peasant societies. Thus in some parts of southern and western Russia bathing is still regarded as a rain charm. In times of drought the priest at the local church is often in danger of being thrown to the ground after the service and drenched with water. In Kursk, when rain is needed, the village women seize a passing stranger and throw him into the river, or forcibly souse him from head to foot.

Bathing has been regarded by many societies, primitive and otherwise, as a way of purging the body and the spirit of sin. Sometimes the mere act of immersion was regarded as sufficient for this purpose, particularly if the water had acquired a reputation for special virtue as a result of some superstitious tradition. Often this reputation was an important vested interest of the priestly caste, who derived a considerable income from pilgrims to specially venerated pools and springs. In other cases the sin was not purged by immersion alone, but had to be passed on to some other unfortunate who was forced to go into the water at the same time. Thus, after exceptional misdemeanours, the sins of the Rajah of Manipur

[174]

used to be transferred to someone else, usually a criminal, who earned his pardon by assuming the guilt of his royal overlord. The Rajah and Ranee would order a scaffold to be erected in the bazaar or market-place, where they bathed stark naked on the uppermost platform. The criminal crouched below, and the water dripping from the royal ablutions was supposed to carry the sins of the Rajah into the person of the human scapegoat. The royal robes were likewise discarded and given to the substitute, and the Rajah and his wife mingled with the crowds until evening in new apparel.

Baptism is another example of the survival of bathing magic into modern times. It replaced straightforward purification by water and, although often thought of as a characteristically Christian sacrament, it has been widely practised in other communities as well. Thus early pagan communities in Scandinavia used to carry out infant baptism as an accompaniment to the naming of the child, and in the cults of Isis and Mithras babies were sprinkled with water at a ceremony taking place during the first few weeks of their life. In Mexico the nurse or midwife carried out a similar rite while speaking these words: 'Take this water, for the goddess Chalchiuhcueja is thy mother. May this bath cleanse thee of impurity contracted in thy mother's womb; may it purify thy heart, and procure for thee a good and honourable life.'

In most of these pagan baptisms sprinkling was regarded as sufficient, but in the early baptisms of the Christian Church total immersion was almost invariably practised. In this there was no respect of age or position, and even the Emperor Constantine at the age of sixty-five was plunged completely beneath the surface of the water. In these early Christian baptisms nudity was *de rigueur*, and to avoid any suggestion of immodesty men and women were baptized at different times or in different parts of the river. Only the sick or dying were exempt from the full obligations of the ceremony, but the washing or sprinkling they received was still held by some to be an insult to God and an imperfect completion of the rite.

Another superstitious belief concerning bathing was that it was a cure for sterility. It was held not only by primitive tribes but as recently as the eighteenth and nineteenth centuries in such comparatively civilized communities as England, France, and Italy. Thus in the *Quarterly Review* for July 1870 the Abbé de Burgo wrote:

Bormio is called the paradise of ladies, because as many sterile ladies as bathe in this spring suddenly become prolific, whence it happens that one sees come hither every year duchesses, matrons, and most noble ladies, without any other malady except the hope of offspring, and never yet has one been defrauded of her hopes.

[175]

Similar happenings have even been recorded from such august and venerable springs as those of the City of Bath in Somerset. Thus when Mary, the wife of James II, bathed there in 1687 she immediately conceived, and John, Earl of Suffolk, erected a splendid pillar in the city to commemorate the happy event.

The more cynical commentators have explained the alleged effect of bathing on fecundity as being due in reality to quite other causes. Mixed bathing was often the general rule, and the public bath-houses acquired in consequence a considerable reputation for licentiousness. In ancient Greece, where women seemed especially enthusiastic for their ablutions, the attendants were all men, and wore very little more clothing than the bathers. Likewise in Germany in more recent times it was customary for those using the public baths provided by pious foundations

Mixed bathing in Holland in the fifteenth century

Hanging baths invented by C. Sergius Orata, from a fifteenth-century MS.

and local authorities always to be attended by members of the opposite sex. In view of these temptations it is not surprising that attendance at the baths could be correlated with a certain rise in the birthrate, and there is probably no need to ascribe any special virtue to the waters themselves.

The ordeal by water is another aspect of bathing where superstition has played a part. A person accused of witchcraft or some other crime would be stripped of his or her clothing, bound hand and foot, and then lowered into the water at the end of a rope. The theory was that if the victim sank he was innocent because he was 'accepted' by the water; but if the water rejected him so that he floated on the surface, then he was guilty. This ordeal was commonly used as a method of trial up to the thirteenth century, and for several centuries thereafter in alleged cases of witchcraft. In witch trials the unfortunate old woman was stripped naked and bound so that the thumb of the right hand was attached to the big toe of the left foot, and the thumb of the left hand to the big toe of the

M*

'Le Bain.' Engraving by Freudeberg, 1744

right foot. Contorted in this way one would feel she would almost certainly have sunk, and thus have been proved innocent; but in the event the ropes to which she was attached were often so manipulated that she remained on the surface and was thus automatically sentenced to death.

The first human baths, as I have said, were taken in the natural waters of rivers and lakes; but as civilization advanced, special structures began to be built to accommodate the bathers. At the same time the magical properties of bathing were augmented by a growing emphasis on its hygienic, therapeutic, and purely pleasurable aspects. The earliest artificial baths probably date from the time of ancient Egypt and ancient Sumer, but the archaeological remains are fragmentary and it is impossible to deduce exactly what they were like. More important examples have been found in Crete and on the Greek mainland, but these likewise were on a small scale compared with the great baths constructed in Roman Italy.

The Romans can be said to have invented bathing as one of the fine arts. The earliest Roman baths, built in the fourth century B.C., were cold-water baths, but they were soon replaced by warm-water baths. These were at first quite simple, and it was not until 21 B.C. that the first of the great Roman thermal establishments was built by Agrippa. Succeeding emperors regarded it as a matter of personal pride and prestige to build ever larger and more elaborate structures, and during the first four centuries of our era Roman baths were constructed of a splendour and magnificence unsurpassed by any later civilization.

'Bathsheba Leaving the Bath', by Hans Memling, c. 1485. Gemäldegalerie, Stuttgart

[179]

'La petite baigneuse', by Ingres. Musée du Louvre

The typical Roman thermal establishment contained swimming baths, warm baths, hot air and vapour baths, a gymnasium, and some-times even a theatre and library. The main rooms were the *apodyterium* where the bathers undressed, the *alipterium* where they were anointed with oil and ointments, the *frigidarium* or cool room, the *tepidarium* or room of moderate heat, and the *calidarium* or hot room, which was

[180]

Claudette Colbert taking a bath in asses' milk. From the film *The Sign of the Cross*

situated over the furnace. The order in which the different rooms were used varied at different periods, and according to the taste of the bathers. It was customary to sweat a little at first in the *tepidarium* in one's clothes, then to proceed first to the *apodyterium* to undress, and then to the *alipterium* to be anointed. Next, after a period of heavy sweating in the *calidarium*, the bather would be cooled by jars of water poured over his

[181]

head—first warm, then tepid, then cold. He was then scraped with an instrument known as a *strigil* to remove the caked layer of dirt, sweat, and ointment from his body, and finally might take a dip in the large cold-water swimming bath, or *piscina*, situated in the *frigidarium*.

Those who took baths simply for health or hygiene usually came only once or twice a week. But others, intent on the licentious possibilities of mixed bathing, took as many as five or six baths a day. The highest patricians, and even the emperors themselves, were no exception. Gordian is recorded as having indulged in as many as eight baths in a single day, and Commodus even stayed in the baths for meals, eating with one hand while caressing some glamorous Roman siren with the other. During other reigns, however, a less dissolute emperor might attempt to curb the voluptuaries. At these times mixed bathing was strictly controlled and bathers were encouraged to use the separate apartments for members of their own sex.

The baths themselves were beautifully ornamented and the largest could accommodate 2,000 bathers at a time, with marble seats for 1,600 spectators. Gibbon wrote of one such establishment:

The walls of the lofty apartments were covered with curious mosaics, that imitated the art of the pencil in the elegance of design and the variety of colours. The Egyptian granite was beautifully encrusted with the precious green marble of Numidia; the perpetual stream of hot water was poured into the capacious basins, through so many wide mouths of bright and massy silver; and the meanest Roman could purchase, with a small copper coin, the daily enjoyment of a scene of pomp and luxury, which might excite the envy of the kings of Asia.

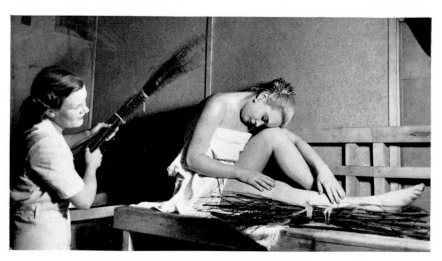

Flagellation of a bather at the Finnish baths in London

[182]

Brigitte Bardot, as Poppea, luxuriates in her bath. From the film *Nero's Week-end*

After Roman times enthusiasm for bathing declined, Britain having a particularly poor record in this respect. One sixteenth-century English proverb ran: 'Wash your hands often, your feet seldom, your head never', the possibility of any other part receiving attention being openly scorned. Even royalty had a bad record of cleanliness. It is recorded of King John that he took only three baths a year in spite of the fact that additional ones were available to him for the comparatively modest fee of tuppence, to be paid by arrangement to his bath servant Aquarius. Queen Elizabeth I was by comparison a paragon of the sanitary virtues, for she bathed once a month 'whether she required it or not'.

Paradoxically the aversion to water in medieval and Renaissance England, as well as in other parts of Europe, was mainly due to the influence of the Christian religion. Christianity as formulated by its founder, and particularly as interpreted by St Paul, is a gospel of asceticism. The medieval church deplored anything that savoured of sensual pleasure and violently denounced the hedonistic philosophy of the later Roman Empire. Baths and bathing came under particularly heavy fire from the ecclesiastics because of the opportunities they gave for licentious behaviour. Cleanliness was certainly not next to godliness during the golden age of the Christian Church.

[183]

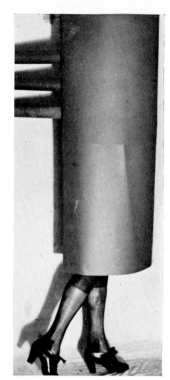

Left: a Finnish family enjoying a sauna. *Right:* a tubular steam-bath of the 1930s

Even animals enjoy bathing, including the elephants at the London Zoo

Yet, parallel with the holy war against washing, certain lively spirits were showing a tendency to relapse into Roman ways. Charlemagne was one of the first to sponsor a revival of the bath, and regularly visited the hot springs at Aix-la-Chapelle. He had a huge private bath erected in the grounds of his own palace, which, far from being reserved for himself and a few intimate friends, was thrown open to his servants and soldiers. On one occasion, the tale goes, a whole company of his guards was found in the bath with him.

The rest of Europe soon followed the example of France. Some of the old Roman thermal establishments, which had fallen into disuse, were restored and reopened, and many new ones were built. The idea of the spa, with its therapeutic waters, gave the idea of washing a new respectability, and the bath was by no means such a symbol of promiscuity as it had been in former times. Many British spas became the centres of the fashionable life of the country, and were patronized by royalty, statesmen, and the most famous artists and writers. The sexes were usually segregated, and if mixed bathing was allowed, nudity was severely discouraged.

During the long renaissance of the bath, which has continued to the present day, several less obvious means of bathing have been devised than simple immersion in water. The Turkish bath, with its succession of hot rooms, became particularly popular, and attracted certain classes of society because of the revival of immorality that took place there. Many Turkish baths were simply brothels by another name, and any woman who was seen emerging from one was ostracized by polite society. The young bloods of the town drifted as naturally towards the Turkish baths as did the middle-aged and respectable to the more dignified and well-regulated spas.

In several parts of Europe, and particularly in Scandinavia, the so-called Russian or Finnish bath has always been patronized by the hardier members of the population. This is commonly known as a *sauna* and is based on the principles of steam heat and flagellation. In the middle of the bathing establishment, which is generally a small wooden structure, a number of paving-stones are heated over a furnace until they are red hot. Water is then thrown over the stones and vapourizes immediately into clouds of steam. The bathers sit on benches round the walls and perspire profusely in a temperature which may rise to 130° F., or even more. They are always stark naked and after some time an attendant scourges them with whisks of birch. The bath ends with a douche of cold water, or by the bathers rushing out and rolling in the snow.

In the East the most bath-conscious nation is undoubtedly Japan.

[185]

Some Victorian and Edwardian baths were almost as splendid as the Albert Memorial

Public bath-houses are an important feature of Tokyo and other large Japanese cities. The bath is always taken in the nude, and men, women, and children are scrubbed by male attendants. All classes of the community patronize the baths, but they are particularly popular among manual workers. The aim of bathing to the Japanese is as much to revive the spirit as to cleanse the body. As one Japanese writer puts it: 'The bathing of the Japanese is far beyond the simple object of cleaning the body; it is so evolved that they bathe to wash their *life*.'

From the point of view of design the most elaborate of all eastern baths were those built by the Persians. These were of a grandeur comparable with the greatest of the Roman *thermae*, and their richness of ornament was on a par with the magnificence of their architecture. Alexander the Great was profoundly impressed by these baths when he first saw them on his eastern expedition, and later travellers have all shared his wonder at their splendours.

During the last century the attractions of the public bath-house have been supplemented by an increasing number of private baths in the home. These range from the ordinary wooden bath-tub to elaborate pieces of Victoriana, as ugly, vulgar, and glorious as the Albert Memorial itself. Far from being a frivolous luxury or a symbol of unchristian licentiousness the bath has become an essential part of civilized life. Although even now occasionally a repository for coals or firewood, its proper value is being increasingly recognized by all classes of the community. To the unromantic it may still be thought of prosaically as somewhere one goes to wash; but to the rest of us it will always be a place where behind doors legitimately locked we can sing songs, think thoughts, and dream dreams. And could there be a better place to contemplate the philosophy of the bath in all its aspects than in the bath itself?

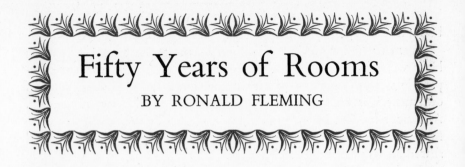

Fifty Years of Rooms

BY RONALD FLEMING

THE TWO WARS of this century have revolutionized our lives and hence our homes. However, our natural spirit of intellectual and artistic expression has not been killed, and in spite of all we continue to live in our various ways in as comfortable and civilized a manner as possible. The interior treatment of our homes is a more revealing expression of our personality and cultivation than our clothes. To trace back, therefore, in what settings we have lived during the last half-century is important to future students of history.

The period can be divided into four main divisions: from 1900 to 1914; from 1919 to 1929 (the beginning of the international slump); from 1929 to 1939; and from 1946 to the present day.

At the time of Queen Victoria's death there were strong nineteenth-century influences still at work, such as the William Morris movement and the 'Art Nouveau' movement from Paris. Soon, Edwardian wealth brought a new luxury, influenced by the Ritz and Savoy hotels.

After 1919, as a reaction to 'clutter', the Regency style was revived, but there were also fashions in Italian and Spanish elaborations—often with disastrous results. After 1930 there was an economical modern manner, with bare essentials in white or beige rooms, but the 1939 war cut off other developments.

Immediately after 1945 any fresh efforts were frustrated. However, as conditions improved, quality work again became possible, modified by simplicity. More attention was paid to heating and lighting; and antiques, if used, were more carefully selected and placed. 'Built-in' furniture, particularly in kitchens and bedrooms, gave efficiency and space; colours were more freely used, often being taken from modern pictures. Many contemporary homes in Britain certainly have an atmosphere of civilized living that can stand up to international standards in design and comfort.

Nouveau Riche, 1900

The drawing-room at Clouds (*above*), built in Wiltshire for the Hon. Percy Wyndham in 1890, shows a revolutionary change from the drawing-room more characteristic of the period shown opposite (*top*), where clutter prevailed. An unprecedented increase in wealth at the turn of the century had brought careless superabundance, leading to internal chaos. Fine pictures or pieces of furniture were largely obliterated by junk. Clouds, however, was a new departure in design, emphasizing simplicity and space, and seeking an atmosphere of cultivated taste. It was built by Philip Webb, and though its architecture was a fusion of many styles, its interior treatment, with the help of William Morris and his followers, stands out as a good example of a new effort.

The treatment of Clouds was certainly more livable-in than the Art Nouveau room at Elm Park, York (*foot of opposite page*). This was designed by George Walton in 1900 and presents a brave, if self-conscious, experiment in advanced design. Art Nouveau, spreading from Paris, started as an escape from nineteenth-century pomposity, and had great influence on architecture and decoration all over Europe. One feels today, however, that it was an artificial movement, lacking in humanity.

The extreme and exaggerated example of Art Nouveau on the left has, for us, an Osbert Lancaster look of the comic, but in 1900 such designs were taken seriously enough. The movement aspired to new designs, without any association with the past. The machine age was beginning, and designers sought to bring a new contemporary spirit into their work. It was a complex and ambitious movement, but it was soon led astray by luxurious fantasy with a touch of 'surrealism'.

The photograph below also has the quality of a caricature. Here we see an example of hedonistic lack of culture. Surely it must be the room of a Poona ex-colonel?

Above we see a contrasting room designed by that great architect Sir Edwin Lutyens. The emphasis is naturally on architectural treatment, based firmly on classicism. His rooms, however, were produced with a personal distinction and a new economy of means. Black shiny walls, a red lacquer cabinet, and a balcony are framed with white enamel paint. The effect must have seemed empty and theatrical to many, but a ruthless operation was necessary to clear away the prevailing rubbish and build afresh. Lutyens was the greatest figure in British architecture and interior design of his time. He was always a keen experimenter, but worked with a scholarly understanding of his problems and with genuine enthusiasm. He was not ashamed to acknowledge his architectural masters, Wren and Palladio, but he chose them well. His interior work was austere and correct, but also essentially personal and uncompromising. There was no clutter here! He provided a sure foundation for interior decoration, though it is doubtful if he understood its feminine aspects of comfort in lighting and soft harmonies of colour.   (*Photo: Country Life*)

After 1919, with the publication of more books on eighteenth-century interior decoration, work by Lenygon, White Allom, and others became more strictly conformist. Work of the highest craftsmanship was produced, but these strict copies of earlier rooms were artistically sterile. They provided a suitable background for establishing a dignified social standing, but went no further. However, individual personality will out, and Victoria Lady Sackville's room, 1920 (*opposite, top*), shows taste. She was an ardent collector of *objets d'art*, and was courageous enough to indulge her whims. (*Photo: Country Life*)

Below, on the right, we see the pine drawing-room in the last house built in the grand manner in Mayfair. Planned pre-1914, but only completed after the war by Lord Aberconway, it had few but spacious rooms. Its architecture was Georgian, but its interior atmosphere was influenced by Italy.

Above is a dining-room in a villa at Cannes created by Monsieur Boudin of Jansen, Paris, in 1923. It was strictly formal, and owed much to its architectural proportions, but it also had individual charm and elegance. The Louis XVI style was strictly adhered to, yet the room lacked pomposity and had a freshness and simplicity in its treatment. The walls were stucco—painted in a subtle manner to represent marble—in soft cool tones of grey and white. Nattier blue unlined taffeta curtains relieved the severity. For the last forty years Boudin has been doing brilliant work in decoration of the finest quality. It is remarkable that France, in spite of two wars, has maintained that 'finesse' in decoration which springs from the eighteenth century. Boudin's favourite periods are Louis XVI and Directoire, and he has influenced taste in these directions.

At the top of the opposite page, as contrast, we see an example of the late 'twenties: the hall of a flat in London decorated by George Sheringham. There is a curious self-conscious effort at originality in the fireplace and settee, and the lighting seems to have been an afterthought! Below is a room in the country in England decorated by the author in the 'twenties. The hand-painted wallpaper, adapted from the eighteenth century, makes a good background for simple furniture, and the room has retained its livable quality.

*Living-room by
Mrs Syrie Maugh
1935*

Mrs Syrie Maugham was one of the most successful woman
decorators between the wars. She displayed considerable flair
with her stripped pine rooms and her all-white rooms. Here we
see her later development, combining colours from modern
paintings with a white background. Her rooms were always
pretty, with a slightly theatrical effect, but her furnishings, alas,
lacked quality. Her mentor was the famous American decorator
Elsie de Woolf (Lady Mendl), who created interior decoration
in America as we know it. On the right we see her tent room
at her Versailles villa. She was brilliantly clever, and introduced
to America eighteenth-century French taste combined with
modern luxury. Below, in contrast, we have a 1929 masculine
décor for Sir Philip Sassoon at Lympne, by Philip Tilden, with
an over-emphatic frieze by Glyn Philpot.   (*Photo: Country Life*)

The world slump of 1929–30 led to modern austerity, illustrated above by Miss Gertrude Lawrence's flat (decorated by the author). Mirror and white walls were relieved with a scarlet carpet and pale grey covers. It made a somewhat severe background for a vivid personality, and any furnishings of quality were sadly lacking.

A contrast is the dignified Regency treatment of the late Sir Henry Channon's house, No. 5 Belgrave Square, in 1930 by Mrs Dollie Mann. Mrs Mann, encouraged by Eddie Knoblock the dramatist, was the real pioneer of the Regency revival after the First World War. Before that the leading decorators, such as Henry Lenygon and Charles Allom, had despised anything after 1800. The spread of the movement was greatly helped by the books of Margaret Jourdain, but prices of Regency furniture remained very modest until after the Second World War. The fine mural over the late eighteenth-century chimney-piece was by that superb artist Rex Whistler, whose tragic death during the Second World War deprived England of one of her great creators of beauty. See also, overleaf, the dining-room for the Marquess of Anglesea. Regency decoration, with its whimsical touch of originality directly inspired by the Prince Regent, proves eminently suitable for modern living. Regency furniture accords well with our traditional architecture, and can be combined with modern comforts. (*Photo: Country Life*)

Photos: Country Life

The mural decoration on the left by Sert, 1930, more exotic than Rex Whistler's below, is a little alien for an English house. Above is an example of decoration by Thornton Smith, 1935, showing his predilection for elaboration, influenced from Italy and Spain. Below, a post-war room by the author emphasizes simplicity combined with comfort and elegance. Oyster walls are enlivened with Pekin Yellow curtains, and the colours of the upholstery are taken from the Savonnerie carpet.

'Contemporary' interior treatment is in keeping with the modern revolution in architecture. A complete break with the past is aimed at, and air-conditioned rooms are designed to be essentially functional. Built-in radios, television, and gramophones, with bare necessities for a servantless age, may simplify life, but surely the atmosphere lacks elegance and distinction? Will future designers be content with such aesthetic sterility?

House at Farnley Tyas: Architect, Peter Womersley.   *Architectural Review*

A GOURMET'S ALPHABET

BY

TUDOR EDWARDS

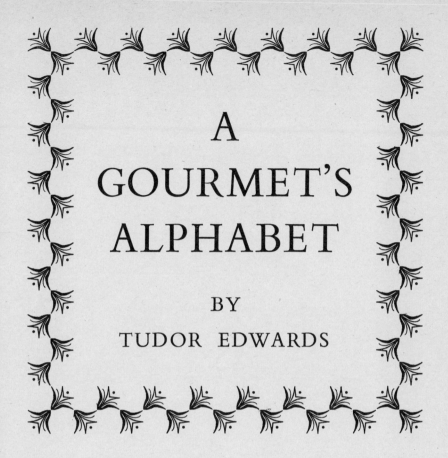

Absinthe, the 'Green Devil' of Verlaine, of the Moulin Rouge of Toulouse-Lautrec and Dégas, of Baudelairean haunts of vice and of *fin de siècle* decadence. 'Bring me *absinthe*,' sang Jean Richepin, 'and let me whirl in a green Heaven with wings as light as a butterfly.' The classic *absinthe* first served in 1797 was compounded of alcoholic spirit flavoured with oil of wormwood, aniseed, hyssop, spices, and herbs. Today it is chiefly made in Lyons and Montpellier, but though it resembles the original in colour and smell, the bottle even bearing the old-style Pernod label, it is no more than a proprietary liquor, and the characteristic flat-holed *absinthe*-spoon has gone. The bottom —the wormwood—has gone out of it. In fact the real *absinthe* disappeared with the Governmental ban of 1914. Switzerland forbids its manufacture altogether, and everywhere else its alcoholic and wormwood content is rigorously reduced to the minimum. The world condemned *absinthe* as the baneful liquor that drove men mad, but has it not provided substitutes which, if more subtle, are equally deadly?

o

[205]

BRILLAT-SAVARIN, christened Anthelme, was born on April Fools' Day, 1755. Magistrate, politician, and musician, his fame rests on one book, *The Physiology of Taste*, the gourmet's breviary. He decreed that in the presentation of food one must proceed from the more substantial to the lighter dish, with the precedence of wines in the opposite order, fundamental rules now taken for granted but then revolutionary. Equally revolutionary were some of his maxims: 'Tell me what you eat and I will tell you what you are.' 'The discovery of a new dish does more for the happiness of mankind than the discovery of a new planet.' 'The destiny of nations depends upon the manner in which they eat.' He was a stickler for decorum and the napkin, but he could be a heretic where wine was concerned and he had an English mania for tea. Sometimes he wrote with his tongue in his cheek, but his enthusiasm was histrionic and he vowed he would not rest until a cook sat at the first place in the Institute of France. To English ears his birthplace sounds curiously appropriate—Belley.

CHOP-SUEY—literally 'mixed bits'. Confucius said: 'Though there may be an abundance of meat, never let it exceed in quantity the vegetable food.' Consequently the Chinese go in for water chestnuts, sea cucumber, bamboo shoots, noodles, water-lily roots, and Muk Yee Fungus, which with the meat is usually cooked in sesame oil. Most gourmets are suspicious of such a hotch-potch,

camouflaged, as it usually is, by a tightly stretched drum skin of egg. Rarer dishes include 'Magnificent Evergreen', a Manchu delight of chicken kidneys and the tender linings of hand-picked bamboo shoots, 'Dragon Crystals', the internal organs of a rare fish shipped from Siberian waters, 'Fish swooning in five perfumes', 'Turnips kissed by the sun', and 'Water angels cooked in honey', not forgetting stewed bird's nest with water-lily nut, sharks' fins, and bears' paws. I matriculated through some of these delights at Chong Choo's in Limehouse Causeway (now, alas, no more), but I have yet to find whether it is really true that the restaurant called the Saloon of the Drunken Moon in Canton serves 'Black cat stew'.

DEVIL'S BLOOD is a strange alloy of orange-juice and chillies with Tequila, the Mexican spirit produced on the slopes of the Sierra Madre. (A brewer in the Shakespeare Country produces Dragon's Blood, a strong ale or barley wine.) From the East comes a potent cocktail called Mee-houlong, which derives its name from the Chinese for 'fire-eating devil'. There is also a Devil sauce containing mustard, curry, and cayenne, a Devil butter, and a Devil paste. Nor should one forget the 'Devils on horseback' (theologically the antithesis of *Anges à cheval*), which somewhat prosaically turn out to be strips of sardine and bacon on toast. Paris has a cabaret called 'L'Enfer', but whether dishes *à la diable* are to be found there I know not.

ESCARGOT should deceive nobody but apparently does. What's in a name? one may ask, but France would not export some 75,000,000 escargots to the world if the labels bore the name *Snail*. Naturalists maintain that there are 1,600 varieties of the snail. Our tastiest is the so-called Roman snail, usually found in copses, and *not* introduced by the Romans, though they are often said to be the lineal descendants of the *helix pomatia*, eaten here over two thousand years ago. In some towns the common garden snail is still sold as 'Wall Fish', and our chocolate-lipped Grove snail is eaten abroad. The Victorians probably ate more snails than we do today, for they were then a common medicine for coughs and colds, and they were also beaten up with milk and sold as imitation cream by dairymen. In France only young snails up to about two years old are selected. The most kingly creature is that fattened on the vine leaves of Burgundy, the most repulsive the enormous orange-coloured denizen of the Yonne valley. There are well over twenty-five different ways of serving snails in France. In Provence there are snail fritters. In Toulouse they are fried in olive oil and served piping hot. In Burgundy they are cooked in white wine with herbs, stuffed with garlic, shallots, and parsley, then grilled. In Languedoc they are served with spiced Montpellier butter or stewed in highly seasoned broth. If you insist upon having them really fresh they can be flown from Paris to London within twenty-four hours. The alternative, of course, is to look around one's own garden.

FOIE GRAS. 'My idea of heaven,' said Sydney Smith, 'is eating *pâtés de foie gras* to the sound of trumpets.' Both the *pâtés* and the *foie gras* are the boast of Alsace, but Périgord has now stolen some of the thunder. The latter, of course, yields the mysterious truffle, that 'black diamond of cookery', but the alliance of the truffle with *foie gras* was created at Strasbourg by Clause, cook to the Governor, in 1762, though this luxury was known to ancient Greece and Rome; in fact one Roman emperor fed his dogs on *foie gras*. The Romans stuffed their geese with figs, but nowadays they are filled with maize. The heretic maintains that the goose's liver is no more than a mere *hors d'œuvre*, but one does not easily forget the little pots filled with a rose-pink alabaster as served in the medieval Maison Kammerzell in the shadow of Strasbourg's cathedral. Equally, one is filled with anticipation by a sight of the *confits d'oi'e* or preserved geese of Gascony, the birds cut into joints, slowly cooked, and preserved in their own fat in tall earthenware jars. By all means cook your own goose and forget about golden eggs.

GRUYÈRE. Pitted with holes like the crater of the moon, this is one of the few cheeses which are wholly cooked, prepared from the milk of cows chased by stocky and picturesque peasants who sing the famous old air *Ranz des Vaches*. It is the chief ingredient of the *fondue*, the large bowl of cheese with white wine and a touch of garlic, heated and stirred, into which all dip small cubes of bread on forks, a messy communal meal which continues until none is left. This Swiss cheese overflows the Jura mountains into France, and on the other side its Italian counterpart is *groviera*. Cheese is more than the drunkard's biscuit. The Swiss store their cheeses so that there are vintage cheeses as there are vintage wines; in the Lötschental there are cheeses that are centenarians. Hard cheese on somebody.

Homard à l'américaine. Bretons, of course, insist that this should be spelt *à l'Armoricaine*, from Armorica, the ancient name for Brittany, but such dedicated patriotism cannot stand up to the facts. According to Escoffier the dish originated in a Nice restaurant, and a Provençal chef, lured by American dollars over the Atlantic, introduced it to the New World. It is also claimed that the dish was first served in Paris in the restaurant of Noël Peters. This is disputed by well-informed gourmets who assert that the Paris Restaurant Bonnefoy was first in the field in 1860 with this culinary triumph. What seems probable, however, is that Noël Peters was the first to serve it under that name. Few dishes have been the subject of so much wrangling. But it is worth noting that Escoffier's classic recipe is eminently Provençal. In Morlaix in Brittany they do the lobster flared with brandy; higher up the coast, at Fécamp in Normandy, it is served with a shrimp sauce. The right way to kill a lobster is to plunge it into cold water and then gradually heat to boiling point, the blue-black crustacean changing to a lacquered baby-pink, as they do in Jersey. ' 'Tis the voice of the lobster,' I heard him declare. 'You have baked me too brown, I must sugar my hair.'

Ice-cream started with Alexander the Great, for it was at his court that frozen delicacies made from the mountain snows were first enjoyed. Marco Polo probably introduced water ices from the east into Italy, but it was Catherine de Medici who took them over the Alps, when she married Henri II of France. They crossed the Channel into England in the time of Charles II, who was reputed to have pensioned his French chef into keeping the secrets of 'cream ice' for his own personal use. By the middle of the last century Italy and the United States were engaged in production on a substantial scale: they have led the field ever since. Among exotic ices is the *paluda* of Persia, flavoured with fresh lime and rose-water. But Naples is the centre of imaginative ices—the *Bombe Napolitaine* and other *bombes* (named after 'King Bomba' or Ferdinand II?), the *cassata* or triple-layered block of different flavours and colours, and those skyscraper concoctions filled with *pistacchio* nuts and fruits. The flamboyant Italian ice-cream carts of one's childhood have vanished, but in the mining valleys of South Wales the numerous Italian cafés still feature a vanilla ice in maraschino.

Jamaica. The island-in-the-sun home of rum, and the first commercial producer of it. Students of Mr Ian Fleming's novels will be well aware of the importance of the product in the daily curriculum of James Bond, when on assignment in Jamaica. Rum—abbreviated from the old Rumbullion, Rumbustion, and Rumbooze—is the spirit distilled from fermented sugar-cane juice. Jamaica rum is the most highly flavoured of all rums (with the possible exception of Martinique), because it contains more esters than any other producer's. Before World War I most of it went to Germany—and the Royal Navy, though it was not officially authorized to the Senior Service before the beginning of last century. But the world has lost its flamboyancy and rumbustiousness, and the old Rum-bullion, reeking of tar, oakum, and fiery spirit, has given way to a watered-down product to satisfy the cocktail-fanciers. Planter's Punch has always been popular on the island, and an excellent version is served at the Myrtle Bank Hotel there. The potent Pimento Dram of the island is a liqueur invented by the Carib Indians, who have nearly died out and are known as the biggest drunkards in the world. The best arrack, a mixture of rice and toddy, also comes from here.

KAVA evokes pages from Stevenson and Conrad. It is a Hawaiian liquor made by the Taupos, the prettiest Hula-hula girls in the villages. Every village has its Taupo; she wears the war dress of the men, and in wartime acts as a vivandière, carrying food, water, and ammunition. She also acts as mistress of the peacetime ceremonies. Kava is made by chewing the root of the pepper plant and spitting it into the Kava bowl. The stuff is strained and served in a coco-nut cup. It is also made by heating the root between stones. Too much kava paralyses the legs, though the head remains clear, and the drinker becomes emaciated and his skin as scaly as a dragon's. In Fiji, where it is known as yagona, the natives drink it as though it were beer.

LARUE, alas, is no more. I was present at the death of this celebrated restaurant in the Place Madeleine, one of the last of the Belle Epoque, on a dismal spring morning in 1954. For the last time one saw the pale golden walls, the Second Empire mirrors, the columns draped with red velvet, the red plush banquettes, and the rose-coloured shades of the table lamps. Here one used to see Senators, dramatists, and celebrities like Prince Rainier of Monaco, the Duke of Windsor, the Aga Khan, Rita Hayworth, Charles Laughton, and Sacha Guitry. The saddest of men on this day were Paul Guénin, maître d'hôtel there since 1907, Charles Beaujouan, the chef who prepared the miraculous caille à la Souvaroff, bécasse flambée, and crêpes Suzette, and Léon Kroll, the sommelier who had the care of 30,000 bottles, including such treasures as the Carthusian liqueurs of 1774 and the cognacs and champagnes of 1838. This was a temple of high cuisine, representing the solid orthodoxy of the nineteenth century. Too many of them are giving way to the cafeterias of our brittle metallic age.

MORUE is none other than salted cod. We may prefer our own homely version, smacking of northern waters and simply boiled, but Gallic cunning has devised some pleasant alternatives. Second only to bouillabaise in Provence is the brandade de morue (which is also a speciality of Nîmes), a dish of creamed cod, reduced to a purée with lots of cream and olive oil, and wonderfully served with grated truffles in Marseille. In Toulon they serve *morue en brochette*, or spiked in small pieces with tomatoes, oil, and breadcrumbs on skewers, and grilled. In Provence *morue en raïto* is always served at supper on Christmas Eve, just as it was eaten by the ancient Greeks on the eve of winter, for the *raïto* is as old as that; it is a rich sauce made of herbs, spices, garlic, red wine, pounded walnuts, tomatoes, and onions. Altogether, cod or *cabillaud*, as the French call it, is a useful fish. The liver supplies the cod-liver oil, the tongue is regarded as an epicure's delicacy, the sounds are generally salted and make a pleasant appetizer, and the flesh (in addition to normal cooking) when salted tides us over Lent.

Nuits-st-georges is a wine-label village in the Côte d'Or country staked low with the grape of burgundy. Nuits is the parish, St-Georges is the vineyard. The entire sparkling burgundy industry began here, and today the Côte de Nuits yields a third of the fine wines of the Côte d'Or. Since the louse called phylloxera laid waste all the Côte d'Or in 1881, the vines here, and indeed in all France, are now a Franco-American combination. Within a few kilometres there is a string of wine villages whence comes the celebrated Romanée-Conti, Clos Vougeot, and Chambertin. At Clos Vougeot is the *château* of the medieval abbots of Citeaux, with its great aisled and timbered cellar and its ancient Heath-Robinson wine-presses, where the Chevaliers du Tastevin hold their gargantuan feasts. Nuits-

St-Georges itself is one of the centres of the *négociants* or wine merchants. The *patron* of the hotel is himself a Chevalier du Tastevin, in addition to being an excellent cook, and he will serve a *jambon braisé au grand vin de Nuits*. This is a fine—but not a great—wine, full-bodied, with good bouquet, one of the princelings of a great sovereign family.

Omelette: a breaking of eggs. Firstly, one should remember Horace: *Choose eggs oblong. Remember they'll be found of sweeter taste and whiter than the round.* There are two opposing schools of thought on the breaking of eggs. Beat the eggs together, says one. No, says the other, beat the yolks and the whites separately. Well, the celebrated omelettes of Mère Poulard on Normandy's Mont St-Michel are made the latter way (and this seems to be the general practice in France), and the advice of that sadly departed estimable cook was given in a few words: 'Very new-laid eggs, the very best butter and plenty of it, a clear fire.' The great Montaigne invented the recipe for Omelette Bonne Femme, and the delicious omelette with asparagus tips was invented by Louis XIV for the delectation of Madame Dubarry. Brillat-Savarin's Curé's Omelette (carp roes, tunny, etc.) is probably the most elaborate of all, while the gravy omelette is a sheer heresy, concocted surely by the Devil. Hilaire Belloc held that he who can make a perfect omelette can probably do nothing else. But don't despair. Blondin even managed to cook one while he was walking the tightrope.

Pêche Melba owes its origin to the meeting of a French blacksmith's son and an Australian opera singer. It was when Dame Nellie Melba was living at the Savoy in 1893 that she asked for a peach and some vanilla ice. The great chef Escoffier (for so the blacksmith's son had become) then created for her a swan carved out of ice, with a peach on vanilla ice-cream set in a cavity, the whole touched up with a coating of jam, spun sugar, and fresh strawberry leaves—the first Pêche Melba. Auguste Escoffier was trained as a cook from the age of twelve. He cooked for the French army in the Franco-Prussian war, worked in Berlin's best hotels, and left Lucerne for London in 1890, arriving with César Ritz for the opening of the Savoy. He went to the Carlton eight years later and was there until 1920. He cooked for three royal sovereigns and was decorated with the Legion of Honour by President Poincaré. Altogether a cook who justified some of Brillat-Savarin's high hopes. Were he alive today he would surely sue many *restaurateurs* for libel.

Quetsch, one of the liqueurs of Alsace, a fiery alloy of brandy and prunes, recalling the Yugoslav *slivovitza*. Others of the region are Kirsch, made from wild cherries, Mirabelle, a plum brandy, Framboise from strawberries, and yet two more based on myrtle and elderberry. These liqueurs can also be found in Luxembourg. It is said that the blessed mixture of sugar with alcohol was invented to warm the old age of Louis Quatorze. But it simply is not true. It was in late-medieval Italy that liqueurs first received

serious attention, and it was a century more before the art reached France. Some fine old liqueurs popular over a century ago have disappeared. What has happened to Liqueur des Iles and Noyeau de Martinique? On the other hand, I have tasted over a score of little-known liqueurs of varying quality made in French and Italian monasteries. The Dutch excelled in liqueurs a couple of centuries ago, and today Nicolaas Kroese, the genial and discriminating host of several Amsterdam restaurants, has revived a number of them, their names a catalogue of intrigue—Jack in the Cellar, Bride's Tears, Eau de ma tante, Pull up your Shirt, Midwife's Aniseed, Consolation in Bitter Suffering, and others.

Recipe for the newly rich. Take a fine seeded olive, stuffed with capers and steeped in virgin oil, and place it in the carcass of a fig-pecker. Place the fig-pecker into a fat ortolan. Place the ortolan into the carcass of a field-lark, with the bones removed and a rasher of bacon wrapped around it. Place the field-lark into the carcass of a thrush which has also been dressed and trussed. Place the thrush into the carcass of a juicy vineyard quail. Place this quail, wrapped in a vine-leaf, into the carcass of a lapwing. Place the lapwing, dressed in a frock-coat of bacon, into the carcass of a beautiful golden plover, then the plover, well larded, into the carcass of a young red partridge, and the partridge into the carcass of a succulent woodcock, tender as a dancing-girl. Place this woodcock, garnished with thin crusts of bread, into the carcass of a teal duck, the teal into the carcass of a young guinea-hen, and the guinea-hen, well larded, into the carcass of a young wild duck. Now the duck goes into a white capon, the capon into a pheasant, the pheasant into a wild goose, and finally place this into the carcass of an exceptionally lovely, fat, white turkey, filling any tiny spaces with chestnuts and a rare stuffing.

Now place your turkey into a capacious pot together with cloves, carrots, finely diced ham, herbs, bacon, fine spices, coriander, and garlic. Seal the pot hermetically with a flour paste, and leave for twenty-four hours on a slow fire. Now! We have reached the sublime in the culinary art. All these juices have intermingled, imparting to this unparalleled dish a marvellous flavour —the quintessence of the plains, the forests, the marshes, and the finest poultry yards. At last the slow penetration of all these juices has reached the heart—has reached the olive! You therefore carefully undo the turkey, which you will either throw out of the window or give to your dogs. By the same route will follow the goose, the pheasant, the duck, the guinea-hen, the teal, the woodcock, the partridge, the plover, the lapwing, the quail, the thrush, the field-lark, the ortolan, and the fig-pecker. Preciously, then, you serve the olive, and, having placed it in the mouth, you savour it long and well. You will find it delectable. (From the *Almanach de Cocagne*.)

SAUCES. Voltaire, in a celebrated gibe, accused the English of having a hundred religions and only one sauce. This is no longer true, though we still steal from the French, whose great sauces bear the names of the celebrities who invented them, among them Bechamel, Condé, and Richelieu (a sauce aptly named because of its red colour and cardinal virtue). No longer are we so insular that we mumble, 'Oh, yes, sauce to disguise poor food.' More often food is ruined by a lumpy raw-tasting billsticker's paste that passes for sauce. The art of the *saucier* is a noble one, but these artists are not above coming to blows like bruisers over a Mayonnaise. For there are two schools of Mayonnaise saucerers, the Hot and Cold schools. The former was championed by Philéas Gilbert, whose recipe is still used, and the latter is best represented by the recipe of the great chef Caréme. The name Mayonnaise is a corruption of Mahon, the capital of Minorca, captured by the French in 1756, when the sauce was invented and named in honour of the victory. The onion sauce Robert dates from the Middle Ages. The white cheese sauce Mornay was concocted by de Mornay himself, friend and courtier of the gay Henri IV; and sauce Financière was invented in Paris's famous Maison Dorée. But, with Socrates, we may believe that 'the best sauce for food is hunger'.

TAGLIATELLI. The ribbon-like *tagliatelli* of Bologna is related to the rope-like *spaghetti* of Naples, the tuberous *macaroni*, the flat rectangular *fettucini* of Rome, and the worm-like *vermicelli*. All belong to the *pasta* family, said to have been introduced from China into Italy by Marco Polo. So do the ball-like *gnocchi*, the miniature mountains of *cannelloni* and the small meat-filled envelopes of *ravioli*. *Tagliarini* are green spinach-flavoured versions of *tagliatelli*; yet another version of the latter is *papardelle*. Again, *agnellotti* and *tortellini* resemble *ravioli*. It is a tongue-twisting confusing world of pallid starchy streamers and fragments. Yet inventive Italian cooks transform this *pasta* into edible joys. The composer Rossini (who married his cook) used a syringe to fill each tube of *macaroni* with beef marrow and then cooked it with *foie gras*, fillets of game, and truffles. In Naples the *spaghetti* is served with a tomato sauce, in Bologna with a meat sauce.

UNITED STATES cookery is rich in all the paradox of the New World. Along the western seaboard there is the traditional clam chowder or shellfish soup, with rashers of bacon fried in butter floating in it. In Massachusetts the regional chicken pie has as many devotees as has chicken Maryland, and one does not forget the grilled chicken New Orleans as served in Antoine's restaurant in that hothouse city. Corned-beef hash and Boston-baked beans suggest lunch break for stevedores. There is corn on the cob, corn fritters, and sweet corn pancakes with maple syrup. There is sweet black bread made of flour, molasses, and raisins. And there are strange salads like the Waldhorf salad of walnuts, grapefruit, and mayonnaise. Some of these delights can be sampled in a London hotel recently built under the banner of the Stars and Stripes. But perhaps the most attractive feature is the rich variety of cool refreshing juleps and the many fresh fruit drinks that can be picked up at booths on the sidewalks. Yet this is also the empire of Coca-cola, canned food, and the refrigerator, all equally abhorrent to the epicure, and of the monstrous food tablets fit only for Martians.

VOUVRAY. From the *château* country of the Loire comes this sparkling flint-flavoured white wine, second only to champagne yet little known in this country. This is one of those ambrosial wines of Touraine which Rabelaise dubbed *la purée Septembrale* —September mash, and it is the wine celebrated by Alexandre Dumas and all the novelists of 'cloak and dagger'. The grapes grow in small vineyards on the sloping hills surrounding Vouvray village, and the wine is brought to maturity in the calcareous caves of the area, caves which are often converted into primitive dwellings and inhabited by troglodytes. Since the wine is made from the *Pinot* grape, the finest and rarest of the grapes, it is never very cheap, since there is never enough of it. It is perfect after ten years in bottle.

WIENA SCHNITZEL. The traditional meat dish of Austria is the *schnitzel* or 'little cut'. No one knows its exact origin. Basically it is fried veal. The three most popular versions have been the mainstay of Viennese menus for centuries—the *Wiener* (or Vienna), fried in a coat of egg and breadcrumbs, the *Pariser*, in batter, and the *natur*, which is simply fried in butter. In addition there is the *Ungarischer* from Hungary across the way, which has a paprika sauce and sometimes sour cream. There is also *kalbfleisch* or pickled veal, not forgetting *goulasch*, a hot stew of tender pieces of meat and tomatoes, of which the even spicier Hungarian version is also available. The discerning will eat these things in Vienna's great Hotel Sacher, with its tapestries and crimson wallpapers, but the im-pecunious *and* discerning will seek out the *beiseln* or little inns like the Griechenbeisel, a haunt of Schubert and still a students' tavern, where they pass round the huge two-litre Doppelkrug tankard.

XDouble-X and treble-X are brewers' names for quali-ties of beer. Xeres was in ancient times the name for sherry. There is nothing else except Xmas Pudding. The Puritans tried to ban this, together with mince pies and all traditional festivities, and the reaction of the people led to the 'Plum Pudding Riots' of Christmas, 1647. The pudding is almost the monopoly of this island; elsewhere its place is taken by various festive specialities. The French have the *bûche de Noël*, a sweet decorated to imitate a yule-log, and there is also the immense crown-shaped *fougasse*, a cake made with rum. In Provence the *Réveillon* or Christmas dinner (eaten on the night of Christmas Eve) concludes with the traditional 'thir-teen sweets'—usually dried grapes or figs, miniature *fougasses*, almonds and walnuts, pine kernels, nougat, milk-cakes scented with fennel, apples and pears, crystallized fruits, *pis-tacchio* nuts, jams, a soft white cheese, buns or a fritter, and dessert wine. Fortunately the following day is a public holiday.

YEMAS DE SAN ISIDRO is an almost Arabian sweet of can-died egg-yolks and oranges, made by the Jeronomite nuns of Seville and sold at the convent door. *Yemas de Santa Teresa* is made and sold by the Carmelites of Avila.

Spanish nuns also make *limoncilla*, a lemon sweet, and 'angel's hair', a sweet with which is mixed strands of pumpkin flesh. The *ovos moles* of Aveiro in Portugal, a sweetmeat largely compounded of egg-yolks and now sold in little wooden barrels in the shops, were originally made in a convent in that town. Such sickly sweets were no doubt inspired by Arabian cuisine, recalling the Arab orange *khòsàbi* (a cold syrup of boiled oranges with added orange and orange-flower water and served with ice) and *sikènjèbin* or marjoram sherbet. But our Anglo-Saxon palates are better trained for a Yorkshire pudding than for a *yemas*.

ZARZUELA DE PESCADO, literally 'a musical comedy of fish', a mixed fish dish that is a good introduction to Spanish cuisine. Those addicted to the sea food of a Prunier will here adventure among *angulas* (tiny freshwater eels), *pulpitos salteados* (baby squid), and the rubbery larger version *calamares*. In the *bodegas* of Madrid, out of the pages of a Pérez Galdós novel, one stands drinking and eating *tapas*, the little snacks which include many fish. On the Mediterranean coast a *Paella* turns out to be another musical comedy of fish, including the squid, all laid on a brown bed of rice. But inland the true *paella* is quite another dish. *Paella Valenciana* is one of Spain's classic dishes, a hot iron dish of meat, chicken, sausage, fish, lobster, artichokes, chickpeas, onion, red peppers, and saffron-coloured rice—the essence of the whole of Spain. It is unfortunate if one does not like cooked rice, for, outside China, Spain is the only country where the art flourishes.

A BOUQUET OF VINTAGES

BY EDMUND PENNING-ROWSELL

THIS last decade is going to be a bad one for wine snobs. Going to be, because it will be some years before the full stature is attained by the remarkable series of vintages over the past ten years. And, for opposing reasons, the anti-wine snobs may feel rather uncomfortable too. For the wine snobs will find that, contrary to the belief that things have never been the same since the '64 Lafite, or at least the '98 Chambertin, in fact we have just experienced as splendid a bouquet of vintages—if that be an appropriate collective noun—as we could wish for. On the other hand, the anti-wine snobs, who decry 'all this vintage nonsense' and toss off immature young wine as if it were Spanish 'champagne', may live to regret the days when they dispatched so summarily their '49s, '53s, and '55s; their like may not be just round the corner in the '60s.

Certainly there have been successions of lean vintages in the past; but a series of poor years would be felt in the years immediately ahead, more, for example, than in the last disappointing decade—the nineteen-thirties. Then there existed a surplus of fine, mature wines. In 1939 one could buy excellent 1920 and 1924 château-bottled claret for seven or eight shillings a bottle. But in Britain alone wine consumption has doubled since 1939, and, owing to the disappearance of older wines during the war, it has been the bountiful post-war vintages which have been drunk up in their infancy.

Therefore those of us, neither snobs nor inverted snobs, who like to drink our wine intelligently may find this a good moment to look back at the vintages of the past ten years, to examine our reserves, and then to try to increase them while still generally available.

It is appropriate to begin with 1949 for two reasons: it is possibly the finest claret and red burgundy year since the war (although 1945 admirers might contest that), and it is the most senior vintage now generally, if slenderly, to be bought. It was also the first post-war year when really good wine was produced in all the main European wine districts; for it was the first year in which the German wines recovered their full form. Champagne did well too, but it was in Bordeaux and Burgundy that the really notable wines were made. In these areas the crop was above average in quantity as well as in quality, and for early buyers prices were low. In a sense what still remains of these wines has been by-passed in favour of the following years, particularly 1953, when remarkably forward, easy-to-drink wines appeared. The 1949s, which in 1951 and 1952 seemed to lack 'stuffing', performed the not unusual feat of 'growing in bottle'. They tasted immature and backward, and as far as claret is concerned that is still partly true today. Yet one of the most reliable of the leading *cru classé* château-proprietors has told me that he believes his 1949 wine to be the finest he has yet made since the war. The more rapidly maturing red burgundies of 1949 are mellower, but even they have plenty of reserves—or the good, well-made, and genuine wines have. They are softer than the '52s, more full-bodied than the '53s, and probably, for it is early days yet, more distinguished than the '55s.

In short, 1949s will repay keeping yet. Those who have nothing older might well give them some years' grace, while for current drinking looking around for '47s or the lesser, but very attractive, examples of '53.

This self-denial does not apply, however, to white wines. Any that are not château- or estate-bottled are probably past their best already, for a cross-Channel journey in cask usually reduces the life of a white wine. However, splendid white wines were made in 1949. Ch. d'Yquem has not produced a better wine since, and white burgundies, when bottled at source, are still very fine. Another district which made exceptionally good wines in 1949 was the Rhône.

The next vintage was something of a freak. The summer was poor in 1950, and during the vintage the rain deluged down. However, the grapes were plentiful on the vines, they were free of disease, and occasional miraculously sunny days saved the vintage; the vats were filled with rain-swollen grapes and, particularly in Bordeaux, a prodigious quantity of wine was made. At Ch. Pontet Canet, one of the largest of the Médoc vineyards, a general average of 200 *tonneaux* (four hogsheads to the *tonneau*) is made; in 1950 the figure was reputed to have been nearer 500. Quantity on this scale seldom leads to quality, but oddly enough the clarets turned out surprisingly well. Low in price and early maturing, they provided admirable medium-quality wines to fill gaps between finer years. But in some cases much more than that. In the St Emilion and Pomerol districts the wines had more body than in the Médoc and Graves; they have still to reach their best, and this applies also to the finer Médocs.

The red burgundies of 1950 were undistinguished, but the white burgundies were excellent. It is a fact that the white wines often succeed in a vintage that is mediocre for the reds. The *domaine* or French-bottled white burgundies are still excellent, although they will not improve further. In Bordeaux the white wines were quite good, in Germany the vintage was large but qualitatively uninteresting.

Nineteen fifty-one has nothing to recommend it. The vintage was noteworthy as being the first in which the Bordeaux growers were legally allowed to add sugar to the must in the fermenting vats; the same applied again in 1954. The vintage was not shipped to this country, but I have had the opportunity of tasting one or two wines, all St Emilions, whose natural robustness, eked out with some added sugar, resulted in surprisingly agreeable wines for ordinary drinking. I have never come across an admitted 1951 burgundy, red or white. That is not to say that none was made; it was, in quantity. Part was sold as non-vintage, but part, I fear, was tipped into adjacent vintages of finer quality and, perhaps, sold under their *millésime*.

In France, incidentally, it is probably fair to say that the name of a wine counts for more than the vintage; in this country the vintage reputation is more important than the name of the growth.

After these two moderate or mediocre years, 1952 was received with great acclaim. The wine was plentiful, and it was good; maybe a little hard and austere, but that suggested *un vin de garde*, a keeper. How good still remains to be seen, for both in Bordeaux and Burgundy controversy continues as to the respective merits of 1952 and 1953. There are those who contend that in both districts 1952 is the better,

the more substantial and well-backed wine. Nineteen-fifty-three, they maintain, is, if superficially attractive, too light and forward, but lacking in real quality or distinction. The opponents of this view sometimes sink so low as to suggest that the opinions of the Fifty-Twoers in the wine trade are influenced by the fact that they had put their shirt and all available capital on 1952, and so had little to spare for the succeeding vintage. The Fifty-Three-ers maintain that the later vintage produced beautifully balanced wines, and that the fact that they are drinkable early in no way counts against them. To support this view they quote historic vintages; for example the famous 1875 clarets which were so light in the early 1880s that everyone was counselled to drink them up 'while they are so good'. Yet the '75s, always light, always delicate, survived well into the 1930s. The same applied to the 1923 burgundies, so far the greatest vintage of the century. As a distinguished wine merchant has recently said to me, 'The '23s were so light and elegant in the beginning that they were turned down by City sharks for that reason; yet they have lasted better and longer than any of the surrounding vintages.' Then the celebrated 1929 clarets were so agreeable shortly after bottling that the cry went up that they 'could not last'. Forwardness is not necessarily a virtue, but it should not be despised; balance is the essential, and this is not an easy matter to assess.

With the '53s I would be inclined to predict a longer life for the Bordeaux than for the burgundies; rather more confidently I would prophesy that the '52 burgundies would out-live the '53s. This may be true also of these two claret vintages, although some experts in Bordeaux hold the 1952 St Emilions and Pomerols to be better than the Médocs, and the reverse to be true in 1953. The only way to settle the point is to secure a good reserve of each vintage—the oldest now generally available on a large scale—and to try them out as they develop over the next few years. What is certain is that both vintages will have generally been drunk up before they reach their best; and a bottle at home is worth a dozen available by hearsay.

A pair of vintages always exercises a particular fascination. When two succeeding years turn out well there is speculation as to whether they will become another glorious couple such as 1899 and 1900, or 1928 and 1929. The double is very rare; whether 1952 and 1953 live up to this hope will not be clear for some years yet.

The Whites particularly distinguished themselves in these two years. If the '52 German wines lacked the completeness and lusciousness of the '53s they are good wines; the '53s have yet to be surpassed in the Hock and Moselle areas in this decade. It is the last year in which the great *trockenbeerenauslese* and *edelbeerenauslese* wines were produced on any scale. Some people imagine that these wonderfully rich, essential wines are made in any moderately good vintage; in fact in the past thirty years they have been possible only five or six times, and then only on a minute scale. No wonder that they occasionally fetch £12 or more a bottle from those to whom this is the consummation of all liquors.

White burgundies were delicious too in 1952 and 1953. For general purposes these are the oldest vintages still in their prime. Indeed, unless bottled at source they have often now lost the freshness and delicacy which are the essentials of fine white burgundy. It is worth recording, too, the exceptional qualities of Beaujolais in 1952 and, particularly, 1953. The latter have not yet been surpassed for fruitiness combined with suavity. I refer of course to the genuine Beaujolais, not the common run which is usually laced with Rhône or other wines.

A descent was inevitable after two such years, and 1954 was not a vintage to write home about—or take home. Some of the legally sugared clarets turned out very drinkable, particularly the fuller wines like Ch. Latour and Ch. Cheval Blanc, both of which I have found fair drinking. Rather astringent, slightly acid white burgundies were made, and a few found their way over here; they were better than they might have been, but very few '54s made the Channel crossing—at least under their own vintage label!

Nineteen-fifty-five has been the

most recent all-round success, and the most widespread one of the decade. The port shippers declared it a vintage, and '55 is generally estimated to be the best port vintage since the war. Cognac was good too, although it will be a decade and more before it appears in bottle. German wines were fair in '55, but owing to poor weather at the vintage, they fell short in lusciousness and depth.

It was just as well that 1955 was a good year in France, for in the following February occurred the biggest disaster since the phylloxera plague in the late nineteenth century. Frost played havoc in the vineyards, particularly in Bordeaux, where the destruction of vines, particularly old vines, put some St Emilion and Pomerol vineyards temporarily out of economic production. Ch. Cheval Blanc, which normally produces about 600 hogsheads annually, made precisely two in 1956. In the Médoc and in Burgundy the 1956 récolte was drastically reduced. Happily the preceding '55s anticipated the gap. The burgundies are so forward even today that they may be drunk up before their successors are ready; the clarets are well-rounded wines. Quantity in all regions was less than in 1953, and 1955 marks the year when a shortage of good French wine became apparent and prices began to rise sharply. They seemed very dear—until the even smaller 1957 crop came along. This was the first recent year, too, when speculators

began buying clarets 'on the branch', four or five months before the vintage. After 1955 the four *premiers crus*, whose pre-vintage price had been abnormally worked up in that year, agreed amongst themselves not to offer their wine before it was made; but lesser growths continued to do so in 1957 and 1958.

After the '52s and '53s, the best buy on the market now are the 1955s, and they are certainly cheaper and available on a wider scale in Britain than in their native districts. The '55 white burgundies have not been equalled since, and this vintage remains the last really good Beaujolais vintage, which was made in very small quantity in the two following years, and plentifully in the mediocre '58 vintage.

Following the sad, frost-bitten, rained-out 1956 vintage, 1957 seemed at one point miraculously good. This was illustrated by the fantastic prices paid at the annual Hospices de Beaune sale in November 1957. This is the first opportunity each year when the new burgundy vintage can be assessed. Whereas in 1955 the Hospices's own vineyards produced 467 hogsheads of red and white wine which fetched 52 million francs, in 1957 only 246 hogsheads were sold for 60 million francs. The eleven casks (each of less than 300 bottles) of the famous top growth, Nicolas Rolin, went for about £400 apiece.

In fact some excellent burgundy, both red and white, was made in 1957, but, as the Hospices figures show, the quantity was sadly short. Moreover, weather conditions at the vintage led to considerable variations in quality. The same applies to Bordeaux, where high, speculative, opening prices later sagged. It is too early to say how the clarets will turn out, but they are bound to be dear, and those with good reserves of earlier vintages can afford to wait and see how they mature. This is true also of 1958s for French wines. A larger, but still insufficient, vintage helped to lower prices, but early opinions on quality are not high. The exception is Germany, where a fabulous quantity of good if not great wine was made; such a flood of wine, relieving the great shortage of Hocks and Moselles, was just what was wanted.

What are the prospects for the next decade, for the '60s? It sounds well, as the memory is thrown back to the amazing series of vintages in the 1860s. But there is no pattern in vintages, and after the unusual run of fine years in the '40s and '50s the odds are that the '60s will be on the lean side for great wines. A British shipper has recently produced a table of 'good vintage years' in Bordeaux on a twenty-five-year basis from 1800 to 1949, as follows:

1800–24	:	6 good years
1825–49	:	8 good years
1850–74	:	7 good years
1875–99	:	5 good years
1900–24	:	6 good years
1925–49	:	8 good years

This makes 40 'good years' out of 150, or nearly 1 in 4. In the past decade we have had 4 really good years out of 10. On the 150-year average, therefore, we may expect only 3 'good years' for claret in the next 15. And there are fewer successful vintages in Burgundy than in Bordeaux.

All of this points to one thing: to make sure of a cellar-full (or a reserve at the wine merchant's) chosen from the delectable decade just passing. It will be the best insurance against disappointment in the coming years. Wine inevitably induces nostalgia, and in looking over the wine lists or cellar books of previous generations one tends to think what wonderful wines they had, and at what fantastically low prices; but judicious expenditure now and a firm lock on the cellar door through the years of maturing should in good time put us on bottle par with our fathers and grandfathers.

BREAKFAST · LUNCHEON · TEA · DINNER

or : All the Human Frame requires

By OLIVE COOK & EDWIN SMITH

THE ECONOMIST,
AND GENERAL ADVISER;
EMBELLISHED WITH BEAUTIFUL ENGRAVINGS.

BEEF.—HIND QUARTER. 1, Sir Loin; 2, Rump; 3, Aitch Bone; 4, Buttock; 5, Mouse do.; 6, Veiny Pieces; 7, Thick Flank; 8, Thin do.; 9, Leg.—FORE QUARTER. 10, Fore Rib; 11, Middle rib.; 12, Chuck; 13, Shoulder, or Leg of Mutton piece; 14, Brisket; 15, Clod; 16, Neck, or Sticking piece; 17, Shin; 18, Cheek.

STOCKING the LARDER

Above: Victorian butcher's shop (Barry Duncan). *Right:* Tea label, c. 1885, and brewer's trade card, c. 1810. The varieties of tea are as distinctive and as numerous as those of wine, and, like the labels on wine-bottles, those on tea-packets should announce the country and district of origin

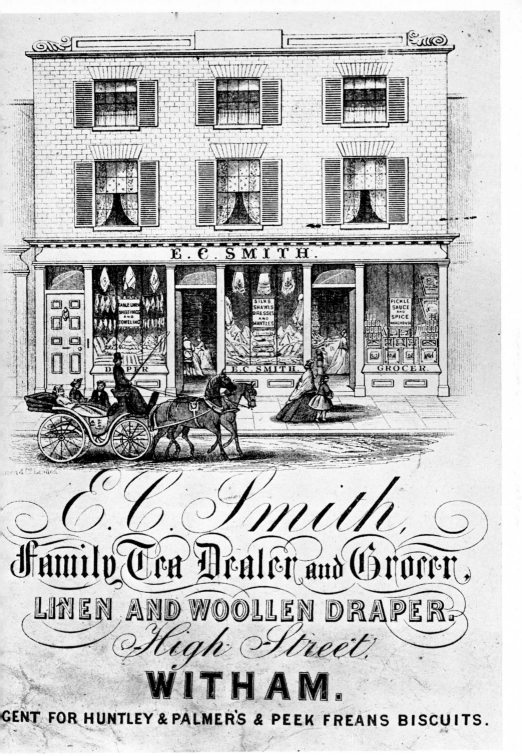

Grocer's paper bag, *c.* 1854 (Louis Meier). Something of the spirit of this lively design with its richly varied lettering lives on in today's soap and detergent vouchers

CALLER HERRIN'

143   Receipts.

To roast a Ham

Take and strip off the Skin, and
let it soak one day in Water, and
two more days in Milk and Wa...
boil it so as not for the spit to ...
out at the fat side, then take 2 or ...
sheets of Tobacco paper, wrap it
in, baste it with nice Dripping
flour, if large it will take 3 ...
and a half or 4 hours roasting

Left: Herring girl (Andrew Bloc
Below: Edith, the Penge m
maid, 1915, and 'Milk Belo
(Cavendish Square). *Opposite:*
Invitation to dine with
President and Governors of
Marine Society (Louis Meic
a Victorian steamer, a precur
of the pressure-cooker; cooking
an open grate, *c.* 1750, and roast
an ox whole at Stratford-on-Av
during the October Mop Fair

STEAMERS

HUTCHINGS PATENT

A Boiler. B Cooker. C Steam Pipe. D Cap.
E Valve. F Warning Whistle. G Filler.

OOKS' TIME TABLE.

BREAKFAST

'Breakfast in the Studio' by M. Duez (1873)

Opposite: Cream jug, *c.* 1760; toast-rack by the architect C. F. A. Voysey, *c.* 1900, and Chelsea-Derby porcelain, *c.* 1775.

Right: The pot, made by John Fawdery in 1704 (V. & A.), reminds us that tea was never taken at breakfast before the nineteenth century and that chocolate was the ten o'clock breakfast beverage

'The Bachelor's Breakfast', 1839

A CHOP-HOUSE.

THE LITTLE DINNER.

DUCKS AND GREEN PEAS (VERY GREEN INDEED).

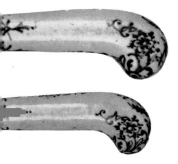

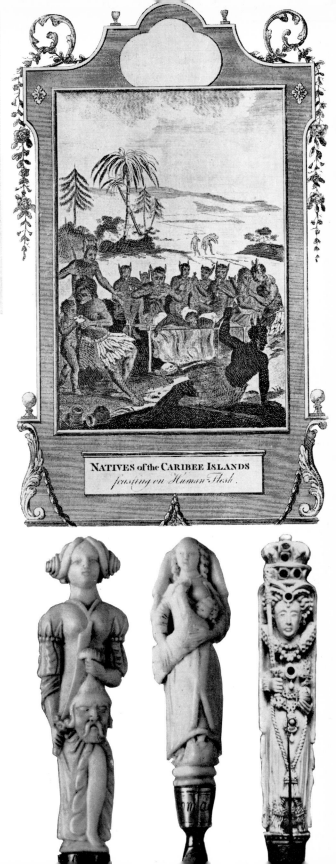

NATIVES of the CARIBEE ISLANDS
feasting on Human Flesh.

LUNCH

e advertisement of the Novelty
nch Room is eloquent of the
anges in the hours of meals.
nch did not exist before the nine-
nth century; then known as
ncheon, it took the place of ten
lock Breakfast.

e ivory knife-handles, *right*, one
which is carved with the figure of
ueen Elizabeth I, are typical of the
venteenth century, while the pistol-
aped handles, *above*, are character-
ic of the eighteenth century. The
rk, early examples of which are
ways two-pronged, only became a
ature of the dining-table towards
oo. (V. & A. Mus.)

TEA

Tea first reached Europe in the mid-seventeenth century, and by 1720 the taking of tea as the genteel finish to the chief meal of the day had become a ritual. Tea did not become an afternoon meal until the nineteenth century.

Left: Spanish porcelain cup and saucer, *c.* 1760. *Below:* Late eighteenth-century English tea-caddy (V. & A.)

Right: English eighteenth-century silver-gilt tea-kettle. The tea-kettle was introduced *c.* 1690 and was heated by charcoal or a spirit-lamp. It was replaced by the tea-urn *c.* 1760. *Below:* Porcelain tea-pot, perhaps New Hall (V. & A. Mus.)

DINNER

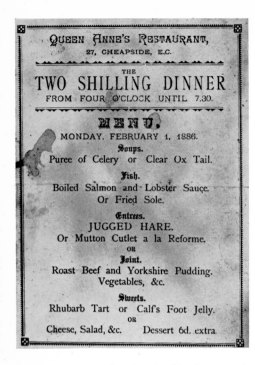

QUEEN ANNE'S RESTAURANT,
27, CHEAPSIDE, E.C.

THE
TWO SHILLING DINNER
FROM FOUR O'CLOCK UNTIL 7.30.

MENU.
MONDAY, FEBRUARY 1, 1886.

Soups.
Puree of Celery or Clear Ox Tail.

Fish.
Boiled Salmon and Lobster Sauce.
Or Fried Sole.

Entrees.
JUGGED HARE.
Or Mutton Cutlet a la Reforme.
OR
Joint.
Roast Beef and Yorkshire Pudding.
Vegetables, &c.

Sweets.
Rhubarb Tart or Calf's Foot Jelly.
OR
Cheese, Salad, &c.   Dessert 6d. extra.

A VOLUPTUARY under the horrors of Digestion.

Once served at three in the afternoon, the hour for dinner was gradually adapted to the needs of the business man and was put off to four, then five and then six o'clock

Above: The Prince of Wales at Dinner, by J. Gilray, 1792 (Louis Meier)
Below: A Japanese steamship menu, 1930

S.S. HARUNA MARU
DINNER

Hors D'Œuvre
Sardines in Oil Radishes   Fruits Cocktail
Caviare au Croûtons   Sliced Cucumber

Consommé Célestine   Crème de Gumbo

Poached Salmon, Oyster Sauce
Braised Quail, Tomato Rice
Fillet of Steak, French Fried Potato
Asparagus Hot or Cold
Boiled Rice
Roast Hind-quarter of Lamb, Mint Sauce
Roast Turkey, Cranberry Sauce
Potatoes, Boiled & Browned
Saute French Beans

Plum Pudding Brandy Sauce
Anana Glacé Dans Son Fruits   Friandises
Gâteau Mont-Blanc   Cheese Omelet
Cheese,   Kraft   Gorgonzola
Fruits,   Grapes   Oranges
Chow-chow.   Assorted Nuts
Café Noir
(Cold)   Roast Sirloin of Beef   Boiled English Ham
Sunday, 12th January, 1930

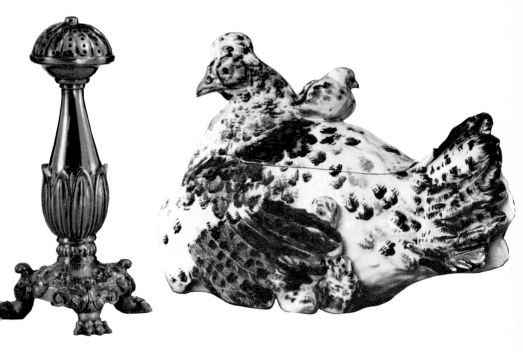

Tureens were introduced in the early eighteenth century and at first assumed exotic shapes such as this of a hen with chicks, *c.* 1755. The eighteenth-century silver caster was intended for sugar or pepper (both V. & A. Mus.)

Below: The Vinolia Works annual dinner, January 1902, at the King's Hall Restaurant, Holborn

Contrasting shapes in drinking-cups:
Above: a Greek cup, *c.* 600 B.C., and an
English medieval cup with green-glazed
interior. *Top centre:* Anglo-Saxon cup and
dish. *Below:* Greek Rhyton (Louis Meier)

A Chinese Ming porcelain wine-cup, *c.* 1430, and, *below,* an eighteenth-century Bohemian double glass enclosing etched silver and gold leaf (V. & A. Mus.)

BRANDY &c. in **1830** we CONSUMED 1,316,770 *Imperial Gallons*

GIN & WHISKEY in **1830** we CONSUMED 22,744,271 *Imperial Gallons*

RUM, in **1830** we CONSUMED 3,653,956 *Imperial Gallons*

Fifteenth-century Maiolica ewer (V. & A. Mus.) Wine-labels first occur in the mid-eighteenth century. The silver Madeira and Claret labels and the Rose Water label, so inappropriately stressing the pleasures of the vine, date from the late eighteenth and early nineteenth centuries; the evocative silver-plated bat design is late Victorian

SNACKS

Top left: Neapolitan lemonade vendor; *above:* 'The Baked Potato Man'; *left:* The Railway Buffet, King's Cross, in 1901, and, *below,* a coffee-bar of 1901

RAILWAY BUFFET (KING'S CROSS).

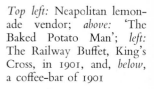

Opposite, top: an Edwardian picnic; *right:* detail from 'SS. Sebastian, Roch, and Demetrius', by L'Ortolano (Nat. Gal.); *below:* an alfresco meal in 1623, engraved on a silver plaque by Simon de Passe (V. & A. Mus.)

The Castle Restaurant, Peacehaven.

AND PICNICS

A FEAST IN A FIELD.

Fact, not Fable.

A lady with whom I once happen'd to meet,
Invited a number of friends to a treat,
I fancy the lady had alter'd her name,
And, one of the party has told me the same.
This occasion'd, for why should the fact be conceal'd,
The feast which the lady arrang'd in the field;
There were many assembled, and every one there,
Felt the bracing effects of pure wholesome air.
And all in the group, both the elder and younger,
Had a certain sensation, akin to sharp hunger,
So a lily-white table-cloth quickly was spread,
With cucumbers, cakes, ham, butter and bread.
Fruits also contributed much to the feast,
And the bliss of the party was further increased,
By the fact, that the stream of the Tea Pot arose:
From the very identical Tea of JOHN ROSE.
Such expressions, as splendid! good! capital! pleasant!
Were audibly uttered by every one present;
The hostess and host were delighted to know,
That the company relished the beverage so,
And happy they were (so the narrative goes,)
To hear the approval pronounced on JOHN ROSE;
For ROSE was the tradesman who chanced to provide,
The Teas which the host and the hostess supplied.
This happen'd in Norfolk, and I had a hint,
To pop such a pleasant affair into print.

Duty on all Teas 1s. 6d. per lb.

Observe, No. 213,

JOHN ROSE & COMPᵞ·
TEA & COFFEE DEALERS,
TEA POT,
No. 213, BOROUGH,
Corner of Union Street,
LONDON.

A Civil War ghost town. Harper's Ferry changed hands many times, to become a no-man's-land by the end of the conflict. Some of the old houses have been brightened by new paint and roof repair. Others remain forlorn and shuttered. All retain their basic pre-Civil War appearance

HIS SOUL GOES MARCHING ON

A Centennial Study by Len Guttridge

1859   1959

YOU STAND on a very high point of land. On your right comes up the Shenandoah, having ranged along the foot of the mountain a hundred miles to seek a vent. On your left approaches the Potomac in quest of a passage also. In the moment of their junction they rush together against the mountain, rend it asunder, and pass off to the sea. This scene is worth a voyage across the Atlantic.' The grandeur which inspired Thomas Jefferson's words has not diminished. The two great rivers swirl and dash from north and south, merge beneath darkly massive Appalachian bluffs, and roll east as the Potomac 150 more miles to Chesapeake Bay and the ocean. But time has added new features to Jefferson's view.

From the same vantage point, after having climbed the stone steps hewn long ago by Negro slaves, I looked down at the Chesapeake and Ohio Canal, a barely visible, weed-choked, and abandoned ditch; its bane, the Baltimore and Ohio railroad, twin bridges linking Maryland and West Virginia; and Harper's Ferry, crouching on the apex formed by the rivers and somewhat suggestive of a Currier and Ives print left out all night in the rain.

Even on sunny days the forlorn aspect of Harper's Ferry may depress some observers. Yet it cannot fail to stir them. It fits the sombre beauty of the region. To me it is most impressive on stormy afternoons, for then the deserted streets are more easily peopled by the imagination with the violent men of a century ago. Their passions, the passions of idealism, prejudice, and raw hate, seem not to have died with them but to have become petrified into the sharp crags of the surrounding hills.

The centenary of John Brown's Raid was but a few months off when I last visited the place. Aware of the sometimes unnerving enthusiasm which Americans show for historical restoration, particularly on anniversary occasions, I expected or feared the utter razing of the abandoned settlement and its replacement by 'an authentic reconstruction'. Every home would be restored, every joist, beam, and nail in careful order, the taverns open and catering (at space-age prices, instead of pre-Civil War), and the menials dressed in period costume. Everything clean, shiny, and new-old. So authentic. So convincingly illusive. And, alas, so *unreal*. This will come about, for the area has already been established as a National Park and its restoration is proceeding under the title of Mission 66.

But not at a rate which can be called rapid. It is obvious that the centenary of the tragedy at Harper's Ferry will come and go before the project is completed. As a ghost town, Harper's Ferry seems assured for at least a while longer: a ghost town, that is, not on the Wild West model, with fallacious legends of marshals, sheriffs, and outlaws made tiresome by nightly re-enactment on television screens. The ghosts who stalk the dark streets of Harper's Ferry were never cardboard characters shooting it out over stolen gold or rustled cattle. They were activated by more complex impulses than greed.

I learned from a National Parks Service officer that the cost of the restoration project far outstrips the available funds. Why should this be? Well, we might consider the ambiguous niche in American history to which John Brown has been assigned. Brave martyr to some, he is

recalled by others as an insurrectionist ruffian. Still others suspend judgment, believing along with Thoreau that Brown was the kind of man 'it takes ages to make and ages to understand'. Since Americans like their heroes to be clearly outlined, and Brown's claim to immortality is clouded in controversy, there has been no headlong rush to provide money for the perpetuation of his memory. Anyway, there seems to be no argument that he was a fanatic. As a boy on a New England farm he vowed to wipe out slavery 'even if I have to carry the war to Africa'.

He left home to begin his anti-slavery campaign in Kansas and Missouri, first as a preacher and plotter, then as an active abolitionist, robbing slave-owners of their slaves. Once he 'rescued' eleven Negroes and transported them by wagon over 1,600 brutal miles to the safety of Canada. Whether from sympathy for the cause or plain desire for adventure, men followed this beak-nosed messiah with the piercing eyes and the never-curving lips from which poured, often without warning, torrents of scriptural eloquence. Yet the final impression he gave to those close to him was less that of a spell-binding zealot than that of a grimly dedicated mortal whose sincerity lay beyond all question. His was an icy fanaticism; and, after he had coldly supervised the massacre by sword of five pro-slavery Kansans, few had any doubt that it was the most frightening kind.

Before the emergence of John Brown the abolitionist movement had expressed itself largely through public exhortation and petitions for political reform. In Brown's view these were ineffectual tactics. While millions of slaves throughout the southern states cried out for release, how could he comfortably attend the debates of the abolitionist intellectuals? The situation demanded action—immediate and decisive; and he had been divinely selected as the instrument. There were multitudes to be freed. God had chosen him to free them. Such was Brown's deep faith, or obsession if you will, and although it drove him to carnage and strife and was shared by few others, not for one second did it waver.

Out of it grew the fantastic notion of launching a rebellion of the slaves. The guerilla activity, the piecemeal rescues, were not enough. Total uprising alone could banish slavery from the United States. His plan, conceived in Kansas and nurtured in the relative security of Canada, called for the capture of the U.S. arsenal and gun factory at Harper's Ferry, Virginia. This accomplished, Brown would arm the Negroes and set up a stronghold of ex-slaves in the mountains.

[243]

The bald facts of the raid are briefly told. In 1859 Harper's Ferry was a thriving little town of some 4,000 souls. On Sunday night, October 16th, outside a lonely farmhouse five miles to the north-east, John Brown mustered his men. They numbered twenty-one, including five Negroes and Brown's three sons. Except for Brown and one of the Negroes, none was over thirty years of age. All wore long black capes and carried rifles or pikes. It was steadily raining. Brown said: 'Men, put on your arms. We will proceed to the Ferry.' At 10.30 p.m. the raiders crossed the railroad bridge, silenced the night watchman, and crept into town, where the guards at the armoury, arsenal, and Hall's Rifle Works were also overcome. Brown cut the telegraph wires and despatched parties to rouse slaves and bring in hostages. Just after midnight, an eastbound train reached the bridge and halted. Out of compassion for the relatives of the passengers, Brown later said, he permitted it to proceed.

Disturbed by mysterious sounds in the night, some of the townsfolk reached for their muskets. By dawn a brisk fire was being exchanged with Brown's men, who had barricaded themselves, with their hostages, in the arsenal buildings. Many men were killed that morning on both sides. At noon the militia from Charles Town arrived and recaptured the bridge. By nightfall the raiders had retreated to the fire-engine house. Only five of them were unscathed. Two of Brown's sons were mortally wounded. A train pulled in from Washington bringing Colonel Robert E. Lee and ninety marines. They waited until dawn on the eighteenth, battered a way into the engine-house, bayoneted two defenders, seized the others, and released the hostages.

In an atmosphere of unprecedented tension John Brown was brought to trial in Charles Town, found guilty of 'conspiring with slaves to commit treason and murder', and there hanged the following December. Five of his associates suffered the same fate. The raid and the trial so inflamed public feeling in the north as well as the south that any spirit of compromise in the disputes between the two was snuffed out, the voice of the moderates ignored. No single event so dramatized the widening breach in the Union as did the John Brown affair. And nothing did more to kindle passions until they erupted into bloody civil war.

The conflict swept to and fro across Harper's Ferry as the strategic heights above the town were fiercely contested. The arsenal buildings were blown up and the bridge destroyed, but the engine-house which had sheltered John Brown's last stand survived. After the Civil War the

U.S. Government displayed no further interest in Harper's Ferry as an arms base or indeed anything else. The town sickened, its condition aggravated by a series of ravaging floods. It rallied briefly a few decades ago as a cheap resort for trippers escaping the summer heat of Washington and Baltimore, but the economic depression and the annual threat of inundation defeated it. After the big 1936 flood had wrecked the road bridges across both rivers, new ones were built a mile up the Shenandoah and a mile down the Potomac, re-routing the highway around Harper's

The execution of John Brown at Charles Town, Virginia, 1859

Ferry by a substantial margin. Thus isolated, its decay was hastened. Today, on the slopes behind it lives a scattered community whose members are not concerned with the deserted downtown area.

It is not surprising that when tourists come to explore, or artists to paint, they converse in whispers, as if in a cemetery, an illusion in part due to the damp odour of decay tainting the air. I last walked the streets in utter solitude, on an afternoon greyly quiet but for a distant song of birds, the faint clang of a far-off locomotive bell, and the eternal murmuring tryst of the waters.

The present railroad station is on the site of the old armoury buildings; a stone marker identifies the spot where stood the fire-engine house, or

John Brown's Fort as it came to be called. The building itself now rests in the grounds of Storer College. Facing the station are the same houses from whose windows the aroused citizens sniped at the raiders. The chipped and scarred façades are of simple architecture; the windows are boarded up, or gape, glassless.

Near the corner of Potomac Street a stone has been erected as a memorial to Hayward Shepherd. The killing of Hayward Shepherd is one of several ironies to be found in the John Brown story. Shepherd was the raid's first victim and a Negro. His master, kinder than most, had already freed him. Locally respected as the station's general handyman, Shepherd died without knowing that he had been shot by the men who came to free the slaves.

Frequent flooding having sapped their strength, certain of the structures along Shenandoah Street sag and would soon collapse were it not for the shoring timbers installed by the National Parks officials. This street contained the town's saloons, where workers from the gun factory, mostly German, Dutch, and Irish immigrants, gathered to carouse and

The arsenal where John Brown held siege: a photograph taken soon after the Civil War

[246]

brawl. They were so doing when John Brown grasped their town by the throat, but not until someone hysterically reported the shooting of Fontaine Beckham did they rush roaring into the street. Beckham was the town mayor and, according to contemporary county court records, a friend and benefactor to impoverished Negroes. Beckham died as he ventured out to reason with the men in the engine-house. Instantly a drunken mob fell upon and horribly desecrated the body of Dangerfield Newby, killed some time earlier while dashing from the armoury to the engine-house. Newby, the mulatto son of a Scotsman and a slave woman, had been saving his money to buy his wife and seven children out of bondage. Only recently had he received a letter from her: '. . . I want to see you so much, that is the bright hope I have before me. If you don't buy me, someone else will . . . the baby is just beginning to crawl. . . .'

Yet another stone marks the spot where Mayor Beckham fell. There is none for Dangerfield Newby.

Near the corner of Shenandoah and High streets stands what used to be Tom Boerly's grocery store. Tom was a fat jolly merchantman who greeted that restless October morning with a smiling curiosity as he left his door. Three paces from it a bullet struck him and he died. I looked out at the tufted rocks in mid-river. On one of these the body of the youngest raider (he was but twenty), shot as he scrambled for its false safety, lay exposed for hours as a target for trigger-happy towns-people until the rushing waters mercifully eased it free.

I turned to the relic of an earlier and more peaceful time, to the sturdy-looking two-storey stone house where dwelt Robert Harper, who came over from Oxford in 1747, bought the land at the junction of the rivers for just sixty guineas, and established a mill and ferry. But it is impossible to escape for long the town's association with violence. Above Harper House stands the Episcopal Church, now a ruin, which housed Civil War wounded of both sides. The stone stairway leading up to it tragically earned the title it still bears: The Bloody Steps.

Half a mile beyond Shenandoah Street are the crumbling foundations of Hall's Rifle Works, captured at the start of the raid, and left under the guard of a brilliant Swiss lawyer named Kagi, with two Negroes. They were soon cut off from the main force. As Brown's 'secretary for war', Kagi smuggled the leader some urgent advice: 'Get into the hills. Our purpose is accomplished. The countryside is terrified and the blacks

[247]

will respond. Pray you not remain in this trap.' Brown read the note in silence. He knew that his purpose was by no means accomplished. He had captured the arsenal but where were the Negro masses he had expected would flock to his banner? They had not responded. He sent word back to Kagi: *Stand firm.* And stand firm they did until routed from the works and chased into the Shenandoah. Furiously swimming, they were halfway across when armed farmers appeared on the opposite bank, trapping them between two deadly fires.

My tour ended with a pilgrimage to the fire-engine house, now a museum in the Storer College grounds, my National Parks leaflet said. It was out of date. The college, a once handsome, now stark, group of buildings encompassing a tree-lined green, had been closed for four years. Bleak and deserted on Camp Hill, originally planned for the education of freed slaves, Storer College today echoes the desolation of the town below. On the gate, swinging creakily in the wind, a sign read: 'Welcome to Storer College, founded 1867. John Brown's Fort straight ahead. Campus Lunchroom open'. It was not, of course. Neither was the administration building, at whose entrance signs announced: 'President Lincoln stayed here in October 1862' and 'Colonel Robert E. Lee stayed here in November 1859'. Most of the windows were broken.

The fire-engine house is set in a far corner of the campus. Peering through the least dirty of the windows, I could see a clutter of dusty objects impossible to identify. It was just as impossible to picture this neat, if unwashed, brick cabin crowded with angry men, sullen men, killing, dying, and dead men. Was it really in here that Watson and Oliver Brown begged their father to end their misery? 'If you must die, die like men,' Brown had replied. When the marines smashed their way in, they found John Brown standing between his two boys, one of them dead, the other dying.

As I walked down the hill to Harper's Ferry, the afternoon sun broke through to brighten the towering bluffs and rolling waters. The town remained in shadow. It will, I suppose, continue to be a place of shadows, a ghost town, until Mission 66 is finished. Then the decay and melancholy will disappear and the town will come to life. But the memory of its far-off conflicts and bitterness cannot be so easily exorcized. A hundred years after, they haunt us still.

[248]

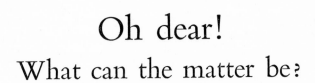

Oh dear!
What can the matter be?

ENGRAVINGS OF THE 'SIXTIES
ELUCIDATED BY CHARLES CAUSLEY

When her sister's stays she wore
Daisy fainted at the door.
It's a mercy Tim, so true,
Knew exactly what to do.

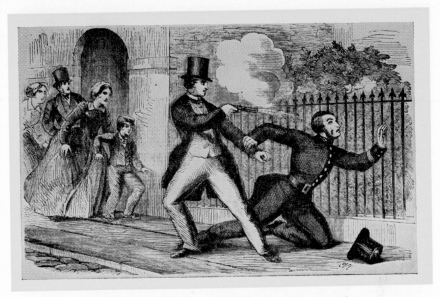

'Pray,' said Mamma, 'don't scream nor scoff.
Actors rehearse on-stage and off.
Their Method now is much more free—
And isn't one Sir Herbert Tree?'

His Lordship cried in accents strong,
'The fish you caught was not *that* long.
Lie there, false heart, to weep and groan.
I'm going to the Ball alone!'

Henry Tomkins—such a swell—
Used to shave beside the well,
Since his spouse, young Henry swore,
Couldn't stand the sight of gore.

'Be still!' called Sam. 'A deadly snake
Is peering at you from the brake.
Hold your head steady, darling Belle.
I'll do my best—but who can tell?'

'Unless,' the Sergeant said, 'you part
And think of Mr D'Oyly Carte
The dress rehearsal will be through
Of *Pirates of Penzance*, Act II.'

Mike Maginnes trimmed his mate
As he cleaned the kitchen grate.
Their mistress cried, 'It is a crime
To cut your hair in working time!'

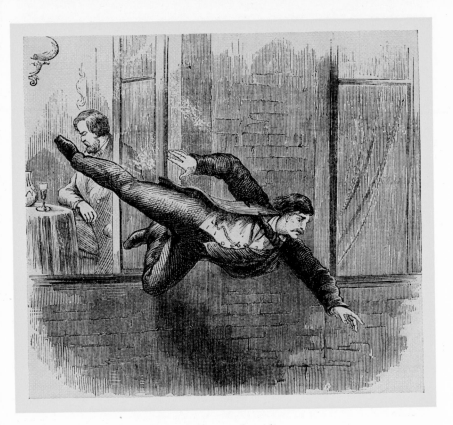

Mad Tregellar used to dive
Fully clad from storey five
And his soul from sin restore
In the swimming bath next door.

This is the house of Lily Logg
   Who bathed at midnight in the smog.
Her husband hissed, 'Give it a rest!
   And cover up your bleeding chest!'

*The engravings in the foregoing pages are
reproduced from issues of* THE ILLUSTRATED
POLICE NEWS *published in the eighteen-sixties*

THE GAY 'SIXTIES

BY PHILIP HENDERSON

HOW OFTEN do we begin with preconceived ideas about the sobriety and self-conscious virtue of the Victorians, only to be astonished by the rowdy licentiousness of London life a hundred years ago! For London in the 'Sixties still preserved much of the flavour of the Regency. 'The highest in the land in those benighted days turned up their coat collars and rubbed shoulders after dusk with others of their species in recreations which, if indulged in now, would be tantamount to social ostracism, of imperilling the "succession",' wrote the anonymous author of *London in the Sixties* in 1908. And he describes himself as one of the Old Brigade—'one of the few who could attend a muster parade of that vast battalion of roysterers, and who, by sheer physical strength, have survived what weaker constitutions have succumbed to'.

But who *was* this hardened old sinner? The British Museum and London Library catalogues describe him as Captain Donald Shaw, the catalogue of the Guildhall library as Ernest Widdrington. According to Mr W. Holden, the author of a life of Cora Pearl, the famous whore of the 'Fifties, who had herself served up naked on a platter at one of her Paris dinner-parties, he was in reality Bobby Shafto, the hero of the well-known ballad sung by the deserted maiden who still believes that 'He will come back and marry me, bonny Bobby Shafto.' At any rate, Mr

The Haymarket, midnight

Holden says that he had this from Bobby's daughter herself. The other candidate, Ernest Widdrington, was also an army man, of the 87th Royal Irish Fusiliers, and the son, appropriately enough, of the Rector of St Mark's Church, St John's Wood.

Whoever he may have been, he was writing nostalgically in old age about the frolics of his youth, when the Haymarket, 'centre of the surging mass of nocturnal corruption', literally blazed with light from midnight till dawn, while at Barnes's, the Burmese, and Barron's Oyster Rooms, they swilled champagne and guzzled oysters in the company of cyprians, those 'divine creatures' from the theatre, so very different from the refined young ladies with whom, at one of the innumerable balls of Mayfair and Belgravia, they had bandied inanities in white ties and lavender gloves earlier the same evening. Indeed, it is a curious reflection on the artificial manners of Victorian high society that men should have been driven for relief to these hard-drinking, hard-smoking, hard-swearing creatures—though what always captivated them was a certain air of innocence, obscenities from a childish mouth being so much more piquant! The whole area south of Piccadilly to the river was, at this time, thick with night houses. As for Panton Street, with its 'hot baths of questionable respectability', it was, the author of *London in the Sixties* tells us, with sly relish, 'the very sink of iniquity and abominations of

[258]

A night house—Kate Hamilton's

every kind'. Beyond the river lay 'Whoreterloo'. To the north, the area between Portland Place and Tottenham Court Road was, to quote Michael Sadleir's *Forlorn Sunset*, 'a low-class flesh-market of a rowdy and scandalous kind', where half-naked whores solicited passers-by from their windows and even ran out into the streets in their underclothes to compel them to come in. London in the 'Sixties, in fact, with its swarming, ill-lit, stinking alleys and narrow streets where the police did not care to venture alone or too often, had not changed very much since Hogarth's London of about a hundred years earlier and contemporary accounts of it fully confirm the most horrifying plates of Gustave Doré's greatest work. Though *London: A Pilgrimage* was not published till 1872, all the drawings for it were made in the 'Sixties, as Doré traversed the whole capital in the company of Blanchard Jerrold.

Another foreign visitor was Dostoevsky. 'Whoever has been to London has been at least once to the Haymarket,' he writes in 1862. 'It is the district where in certain streets at night the prostitutes gather in their thousands. The street is festooned by gas jets in a way of which at home we have no conception. At every step there are superb cafés all gilt and glass. You meet your friends there—and you take refuge there. It is painful to mix with the crowd. Its composition is so strange. You find there old women and beauties at whom you gaze, dazzled. Nowhere in

[259]

the world is there a type of woman as beautiful as the English. The dense crowd moves with difficulty. The pavement does not suffice for it and they invade the road. They are all thirsty for prey and recruit the first-comer with complete cynicism. Grand clothes rub shoulders with rags; the same contrast in age; everything is mixed up. You hear curses, quarrels, shouts, and the engaging whisper of a lovely girl who has not yet lost her shyness. . . . In the Haymarket I have seen mothers putting their little daughters up for sale. Children of twelve seize your arm and want to follow you.' Indeed, the traffic in children (both boys and girls) was most profitable in Victorian times, and increased to an appalling extent, with recognized houses for juvenile prostitutes, until exposed by W. T. Stead in his *Maiden Tribute of Modern Babylon*, the famous series of articles published in *The Pall Mall Gazette* in the 'Eighties. In order to prove to a doubting world that it went on, Stead bought a little girl of thirteen himself from her mother, took her to a bawdy house, and then had himself arrested.

Taine also visited England in the same year as Dostoevsky and his *Notes Sur L'Angleterre* leaves exactly the same impression. 'The spectacle of debauchery in this country,' he writes, 'leaves one with an impression of nothing but degradation and misery. Nothing brilliant, bold, and smart, as in France.' But the women, he has to admit, are very beautiful, though they have no taste. At one fashionable gathering he sat beside 'a young woman whose neck and shoulders seemed made of snow, or rather mother o' pearl: this extraordinary whiteness is so superlative that, to my eyes, it is not alive. Pink dress, a crown of red flowers, green trimmings: they rarely have any sense of colour. Several of the ladies had their hair full of diamonds and their shoulders, fully displayed, had that dazzling whiteness which I mentioned above: the petals of a lily or the sheen of white satin are nothing to it.'

At that time men's tastes were tacitly assumed to be gross and their womenfolk charitably made allowances for it. For the pleasures of the 'Sixties still included cock-fighting, prize-fighting, ratting, and such sport as that indulged on a never-to-be-forgotten occasion by the Marquis of Hastings when he let loose a whole sackful of sewer rats at Mott's ballroom in Foley Street. The marquis, we learn from *London in the Sixties*, was the chief culprit in every sort of devilry. Beloved of policeman and publican, he occupied a privileged position. 'His advent at a ratting match or a badger drawing was a signal for every loafer that the hour of his thirst was ended, and that henceforth "the Markis" was in the chair. . . . Six cases of champagne invariably formed the first order, and as old Jimmy Shaw shouted " 'Ere, more glasses there, and dust a chair for 'is Lordship",

Gustave Doré: 'A Ball at the Mansion House'

the four-ale bar closed in, as it were, and duke and dustman hobnobbed and clinked glasses with a deferential familiarity unknown in these levelling days.' Ratting, particularly, was a favourite pastime of young bloods. Jimmy Shaw, a cadaverous individual dressed like a gamekeeper, was the professional rat-catcher who traversed the main drains half the day, and supplied the various sporting haunts with thousands of rats nightly. 'If a dog was backed to kill a thousand rats in a specified time the supply never failed to be equal to the demand, despite the hundreds that were pitted nightly against ferrets, or produced at so much a dozen for young bloods to try their dogs on. To see this rat-catcher plunge his hand into a sack full of huge and ferocious sewer rats and, extracting them one by one by the tail, count the required amount into the pit, was a sight beyond description, as legislators, Cabinet Ministers, peers, and army men threw sovereigns at him in payment.' The subterranean Cockpit in Endell Street was the scene of these grisly revels.

Grislier still was the habit of rounding off the night's pleasure by going to see a public execution at Newgate—a pastime that attracted the nobility as well as the scum of the population, one nobleman, in fact, posing as hangman's assistant on numerous occasions. Going to a hanging in the 'Sixties was as recognized a custom as the more modern fashion of making up a party to go to the Boat Race, and the prices paid for a window giving a good view of the scene were enormous, varying from twenty to fifty guineas. That scene, as the dense crowds waited throughout the night, drinking and roaring songs, recalls Doré's most romantically gloomy engravings. 'A surging mass, with here and there a flickering torch, rolled and roared before one; above this weird scene arose the voices of men and women, shouting, singing, blaspheming, and as the night advanced and the liquid gained firmer mastery, it seemed as if hell had delivered up its victims. To approach the window was a matter of danger; volleys of mud immediately saluted one, accompanied by more blaspheming and shouts of defiance. It was difficult to believe that one was in the centre of a civilized capital that vaunted its religion, and yet meted justice in such a form.'

The excitement grew when, towards dawn, workmen appeared and began to set up the scaffold. Presently a decrepit old man made his appearance and gingerly tested the drop. This was Calcraft the hangman. He was greeted with yells of execration. 'Roofs, windows, church-rails, and empty vans—all were pressed into service and tightly packed with human beings eager to catch a glimpse of seven fellow-creatures on the last stage of life's journey.' When it rained, as it frequently did, sand was thrown on to the scaffold so that 'the ordinary', or minister of religion, who offered consolation to the condemned at 8 a.m. and breakfasted at nine, should not slip on to the drop by mistake. A dead silence fell as the condemned appeared at last—'a sickly, cadaverous mob securely pinioned and literally as white as marble'. These were the seven Flowery Land pirates, executed in '64, whose hanging created a stir rarely equalled before or since. After it was all over the crowd would take up once more the savagely ironical refrain 'CALCRAFT! CALCRAFT! HE'S THE MAN!' while pickpockets and highwaymen reaped a rich reward in watch-chains, tie-pins, pocket-books, and cuff-links. One party of young guardsmen, arriving late, were forced to descend from their cab and stripped to their shirts in Newgate Lane.

Wherever one went in London at this time fights seemed to break out at a moment's notice. At the Pic in Piccadilly Circus hat-smashing was the thing, and once a tall hat was smashed it lost all its prestige value. The dinner in celebration of Shakespeare's tercentenary in 1864 developed into an almighty scrimmage. Though the spirit of the bard had been

Engraving from the *Illustrated Police News*

invoked at the beginning of the proceedings, a less exalted spirit soon began to dominate the assembly in the banqueting hall of the Freemasons tavern, as potations were drunk to his memory by all those who could claim to be patrons of the drama. Soon practical jokes were in full swing, and serious trouble started when some scene-shifters with voracious appetites began sending their plates up for more and more ham and the wags who were serving piled them indiscriminately with meat, custards, oranges, and marmalade. At this the blood of the fraternity of carpenters rose, and soon dishes and plates were flying in all directions. Even the waiters joined in. 'Wait till I give this —— 'is grub,' growled one, 'and then I'll let you know!'

But the 'Sixties offered more civilized pleasures than these. Summer

Gustave Doré: 'A Summer Evening at Greenwich'

evenings might be spent in the company of some houri at the Trafalgar
or Ship Tavern at Greenwich, where a dinner of seven courses of fish
might be eaten. One would not take a 'lady' there, of course, any more
than one would take her to the theatre and still less to the music hall,
which catered exclusively for the grosser tastes of the male, for here the
chorus 'was selected for perfection of form rather than perfection of

[264]

voice'. Ladies went to the Opera to hear Offenbach, where they evidently far outnumbered the men, who were doubtless otherwise engaged. The 'Sixties was the great age of the Alhambra, whose domes and white-fretted façade some of us may remember glittering through the trees on the east side of Leicester Square, where now stands the giant shiny black box of the Odeon. Here was to be met Alfred Paget, 'a septuagenarian lord who, when not in attendance at Court, as was supposed, seemed to spend his declining years in wandering from one green room to another. Harmless to a degree, it was pitiable to see the dyed old sinner chewing a cigar and indulging in such antics as an occasional double shuffle with any chorus girl he had selected for his attention.' The Maharajah Duleep Singh was also 'in nightly attendance'. He invariably came armed with presents for the chorus. 'What nice little girl is going to have this?' he would enquire, with a roving eye. He finally settled his affections on pretty Polly Ash, who shortly retired into a sumptuous flat in Covent Garden, with a handsome annuity, derived from the labours of starving Indian peasants. 'History does not make it quite clear whether any of the fair members were eventually translated to the Upper House', writes One of the Old Brigade, 'but whether as fortunate in this respect as Mott's, and in later years the Gaiety, it was undeniable that no more beautiful bevy of women were to be found than the representatives of the drama at the Alhambra in those long-ago days.'

But 'going to the theatre' sometimes involved wading through alleys and side-streets none too safe after dark to visit the old Prince of Wales in a slum off the Tottenham Court Road, a theatre run by Colonel Valentine Baker. This was the cavalry officer whose unsuccessful attempt to seduce a young lady in the first-class carriage of a non-stop train from Woking to Waterloo not only gave rise to one of the most famous of Victorian scandals, but resulted in the institution of corridor carriages to safeguard the virtue of solitary lady travellers. In this case the lady only saved herself from a worse fate than death by opening the carriage door and standing with one foot on the running-board and threatening to throw herself out should the colonel attempt to touch her again. It was much safer for military men to confine themselves to chorus girls. At the Surrey music hall, for instance, might have been found, in the pantomime season, 'such goddesses as Val Reece, Lardy Wilson, and a score of others, many of whom have since swelled the pages of *Debrett* and similar works of our religion'. But it was Astley's Amphitheatre in the Westminster Bridge Road that provided the chief sensation of the 'Sixties, when the tough American equestrienne Adah Dolores Menken rode nightly round the ring in the scantiest of shifts bound to the back of a great black horse in what was known as the Mazeppa Act. On October 3, 1864, Astley's presented 'Lord Byron's Celebrated Drama of *Mazeppa*, with a Grand Stud of Forty Horses, Two Hundred Soldiers, and a Superb Ballet'. What Byron had to do with it is not quite clear, though Dickens was one of the men of letters who tried but failed to get a seat, till Dolores herself put a box at his disposal. Tennyson, too, found it hard to keep away, and as for Swinburne, as he watched the athletic beauty wielding her long whip, she seemed to him the very incarnation of his Lady of Pain. The story goes that Rossetti rather wickedly gave Dolores ten pounds to make a man of the little poet with fluttering hands and that she later returned it as unearned. Whether true or not, Dolores certainly became intimate with Swinburne, chiefly because she hoped he would help her to get her poems published, though Swinburne is reported to have told her that 'a woman with such beautiful legs as she had should not worry her head about poetry'. Years later some verses called 'Dolorida' that he had written for her album appeared over his name in a Christmas annual:

> Combien de temps, dis, la belle,
> Dis, veux-tu m'être fidèle?
> Pour une nuit, pour un jour,
>   Mon amour!

> L'amour nous flatte et nous touche
> Du doigt, de l'œil, de la bouche,
> Pour un jour, pour une nuit,
>   Et s'enfuit.

Another favourite resort and meeting-place was the Burlington Arcade. 'Here every afternoon, between six and seven, throngs composed of all that made up the pomp and vanity of this wicked world disported themselves,' writes the incorrigible member of the Old Brigade. 'Here Baby Jordan and "Shoes"—since become the mother of a present-day baronet—Nelly Fowler and Nelly Clifton held court with their attendant esquires and lords of every degree. Here at seven the entire mass surged towards the Blue Posts in Cork Street and indulged in champagne and caviare toast.' The famous cyprian 'Skittles'—to whom Wilfred Scawen Blunt wrote his *Love Sonnets of Proteus*, was frequently to be seen dining at the Berkeley with her worshippers, and it was here that she was once overheard to say to a clumsy waiter who had splashed her with gravy: 'You infernal lout! If I wasn't a lady I'd smack your ugly face!' But chief among the cyprians of that time was sweet Nelly Fowler, the undisputed Queen of Beauty of those days. 'This beautiful girl,' we read,

Gustave Doré: 'The Ladies' Mile'

'had a natural perfume so delicious, so universally admitted, that love-sick swains paid large sums for the privilege of having their handkerchiefs placed under the goddess's pillow, and sweet Nelly pervaded—in spirit, if not in the flesh—half the clubs and drawing-rooms of London.' And all these houris might be seen any afternoon driving in the Park in their elegant equipages, or, in the morning, riding in faultless habits in the Ladies' Mile in the company of duchesses and débutantes.

At Kate Hamilton's, the great underground night house between Piccadilly Circus and Leicester Square, one encountered only the upper crust (or rather, sugar icing) of the profession. They went there, says Bracebridge Hemyng in the section on 'Prostitution in London' in that volume of Mayhew that is still kept under lock and key at the London Library, 'not only to dissipate ennui, but with a view to replenishing an exhausted exchequer: for as Kate is careful as to whom she admits into her rooms—men who are liable to spend and come with avowed intention of spending . . . these supper rooms are frequented by a better set of men and women than perhaps any in London'—money, of course, being the only criterion. As for Kate Hamilton herself, writes one of her old customers, 'she weighed at least twenty stone and had as hideous a physiognomy as any weather-beaten Dover pilot. Seated on a raised platform, with a bodice cut very low, this freak of nature sipped champagne steadily from midnight until daylight and shook like a blancmange every time she laughed.' Yet young men were flattered when she drank their health, regarding it as a sign that they had passed muster as gay dogs and men-about-town. Indeed, comments Hemyng with perhaps unconscious humour, 'it is frequently a matter of surprise amongst the friends of a gentleman of position and connection that he exhibits an invincible distaste to marriage. If they were acquainted with his private affairs their astonishment would speedily vanish.'

Engraving from the *Illustrated Police News*

Gustave Doré: 'The Stalls, Covent Garden'

The author of *London in the Sixties*, if he really was Bobby Shafto, does not appear to have been in a hurry to marry either. He sighs nostalgically not only for the vanished beauties of that time, but also for the vanished chops, steaks, welsh rarebits, marrow bones, and mealy potatoes once to be had in the solid comfort of such hostelries as the Guildhall Tavern, the Albion, Evans's, and Simpsons. 'To see a genuine old English waiter crumble a huge potato with a spotless napkin creates a pang when one thinks of his German and Italian prototype asking: " 'Ow many breads you have?" ' At Evans's in Covent Garden, which catered for a regular clientele, no bills were ever presented—'all the reckoning was one's own as one imparted it on leaving to the most courteous of butlers at the door'. Lane's in St Alban's Place, however, was patronized by the rowdier class of youngsters, with a sprinkling of permanent residents in various stages of delirium tremens. 'Dirty and apparently never swept, the rooms might be described as cosy. The beds, however, were scrupulously clean . . . as the majority of the lodgers spent a considerable portion of their existence between the sheets. . . . Here the ruling spirit was "Old John", an octogenarian in shiny snuff-coloured tail suit and slippers, who apparently never slumbered nor slept, and

Gustave Doré: 'Blondin at Shoreditch'

whom no human eye had ever seen otherwise attired. Assisted by two youngsters of fifty—Charles and Robert—this extraordinary trio knew the habits and tastes of everyone, not that eating was extensively indulged in; and beyond the best joints for dinner, and bacon and eggs for breakfast, the staple consumption for all day and all night might briefly be described as brandy-and-soda, rum-and-milk, whilst the more sedate confined themselves to sherry and bitters before breakfast, and a glass of brandy in their tea. How human nature stood such persistent floodings of the system seems beyond comprehension, yet nothing seemed to occur beyond revellers being periodically chaperoned to bed, and now and then an ominous long box being smuggled upstairs and one hearing a day or so after that "the Captain had had his last drink".'

Then there was the Octagon Room at the Ship and Turtle in Leadenhall Street, where milk-punch was a speciality and 'incomparable turtle soup and turtle steaks, the saddle of mutton one felt it a sin to mutilate, and the honest English pancakes washed down with port—fifty years old—and champagne in magnums'. Here parties used to assemble for an early supper before climbing into their private omnibus that was to take them eastwards to the pantomime at the Grecian music hall in the City Road. Normally, of course, this was an area one did not visit, except with police protection, though emaciated spectres not infrequently emerged from it to haunt the streets of the West End.

'How long is it since gentlemen of the highest degree went to the Cider Cellars and the Coal Hole?' asks Blanchard Jerrold in his chapter 'London at Play', congratulating himself in the early 'Seventies on the general reformation of manners. 'A dirty stifling underground tavern in Maiden Lane . . . was the meeting-place of bloods from Fops' Alley, after the opera. The Cave of Harmony was a cellar for shameful song-singing where members of both Houses, the pick of the universities, and the bucks of the Row, were content to dwell in indecencies for ever. When there was a burst of unwonted enthusiasm, you might be certain that some genius of the place had soared to a happy combination of indency with blasphemy. . . . In those days cellars and shades and caves were the chosen resorts of roystering spirits of all degrees. Under the harmless wool work of Miss Linwood in Leicester Square were cavernous spaces devoted to the late orgies of men of fashion'—a practice resuscitated, one gratefully recollects, by the Late Joys in that Albemarle Street cellar which relieved some of the dreariness of the last war.

In the 'Sixties tobacconists, too, were more convivial places, 'where every afternoon such men as Lord William Lennox, Lord Huntgingtower, Mr George Payne, the Marquis of Drogheda, Lord Henry Loftus, and

Gustave Doré: 'Afternoon in the Park'

Colonel Fitzgerald might be seen seated on tobacco tubs and cigar chests, smoking big cigars and drinking sherry, which flowed from casks around the shop. . . .'. But Mayfair also provided *maisons de convenance*, discreet meeting-places, where it was not unknown for even husbands and wives to meet, accidentally, to their horror.

Meanwhile to the west, in semi-rural Kensington, between the gardens of the Royal Horticultural Society and the trim expanses of Kensington Gardens, the playground of the innocent in those pre-Freudian days, the Prince Consort's plan for a great hall of the arts and sciences was being realized as the northern point of that *cité universitaire* he had planned for this area. But, as the Queen disarmingly confessed when the plans for the Albert Hall were presented for her approval: 'I have no taste. I always follow him'—he who sits plated in triple gold, his pious head bowed above the catalogue of the Great Exhibition in his pink and gilt and azure memorial, surrounded by musicians, sculptors, poets, and scientists and topped by those bronze-gilt statues of the moral virtues which many people continue to associate with the Victorian age.

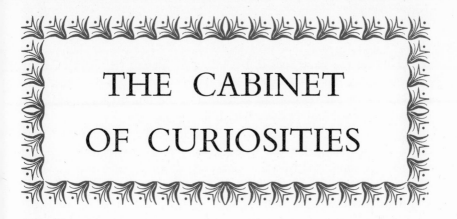

THE CABINET
OF CURIOSITIES

THE WORLD OF RENÉ MAGRITTE

BY E. L. T. MESENS

IN THE MIDST of the Cubist development (1911), when Picasso's and Braque's earlier achievements had stimulated theoreticians like Albert Gleizes and Jean Metzinger to formulate theories on the validity of 'synthesis in representation' introduced by this new aesthetic, there suddenly appeared a sharply contrasting figure, Giorgio de Chirico. Guillaume Apollinaire, the herald of *l'Esprit nouveau*, called him 'the most astonishing painter of the young generation', and added:

> . . . I really don't know to whom I could compare Giorgio de Chirico. The first time I saw his canvases I instinctively thought of Rousseau le Douanier, particularly for the religiosity with which he paints his skies. But today I must recognize that this is a haphazard comparison; before anything else de Chirico is an artist perfectly aware of what he does. He knows more than one way to *see* and to *paint*. Very much may be expected from him.

In his work of that time Chirico diametrically opposed the Cubists, and reintroduced a conventional type of perspective (perspective which had been gradually lost by the post-impressionist and Fauves painters). He used objects and landscapes classic in conception and executed in a simplified Renaissance technique, giving the illusion of reality.

Less than fifteen years later, a similar situation recurred. Piet Mondrian, with his Dutch 'Neo-plasticism', occupied the most advanced position in the plastic arts in Paris (obviously influencing Fernand Léger, Le Corbusier, Herbin, and others). His colleague Theo Van Doesburg was

preaching on the same lines in Berlin and in Dessau (Bauhaus). Among painters in Belgium there was a tendency towards a type of Constructivism (a weak display compared with that of the Dutch 'Neo-plasticians') aiming to put painting at the service of architecture.

In the midst of this stream of theorizing Magritte appeared, very discreetly, searching for the 'poetic', as opposed to the 'rational'. He was happily supported by a few poets whose intelligence and awareness could easily confound the democrat-materialism of the self-styled Constructivists.

It is true that at the same time, in Paris, some painters and sculptors like Max Ernst, Man Ray, and Hans Arp had been switching from the negative Dada-dance to a Surrealist revolution and experiments in psychic automatism. They were soon joined by remarkable men like André Masson, the fanciful genius Joan Miró, and later Yves Tanguy. However, Magritte remained unique in his quest: he alone sought to endow images of reality with poetry without over-emphasis of painter's artifice.

This particular contribution of Magritte's has been acknowledged by André Breton in *Genèse et Perspective artistiques du Surréalisme:*

> Deliberately, and therefore in the opposite sense to automatism, Magritte contributed support at this point to Surrealism from another angle. The only one to pursue this course, he approached painting in the spirit of 'object-lessons', and from this point of view put the visual image systematically on trial, stressing its weaknesses and demonstrating the subordinate character of figures of speech and thought.

René Magritte was born in 1898 at Lessines, a small industrial city in the Belgian province of Hainaut. He drew and painted in water-colours from early childhood. He did not complete his secondary studies but, for two or three years, he followed without great enthusiasm the courses of the Académie des Beaux-Arts in Brussels. At the end of this period he had his first exhibition (1920) with another young painter with whom he had been sharing a studio. It was at this first exhibition that I met Magritte, who is five years my senior. We became friends at once.

His paintings, very daring to my inexperienced eyes, were influenced (it seemed) in turn, and sometimes jointly, by Fauvism, Cubism, and Futurism.

Life was very hard for the painter in those days, and, as he married very young, he was compelled to work for some time as a designer

[274]

in a wallpaper factory. This work was so tedious to him that he decided to become a free-lance poster-painter. He also occasionally drew covers for sheet-music publishers.

A few years later the work of Giorgio de Chirico became known to Magritte, but only through photographic reproductions in art magazines. This was for him (as it was for me at the same time) a significant experience: it moved him profoundly, and suddenly showed him the path along which he was to discover himself.

For hardly more than one year Magritte was under Chirico's spell, but not under his formal influence—as has been the case for Carlo Carrá and most painters of the Italian *Scuola metafisica*, or for the French painter Pierre Roy. From the end of 1925 to the spring of 1927 Magritte made some fifty paintings and a dozen 'collages' (I do not know many drawings of this period—and he painted no gouaches at all) in which common or unusual objects or personages are brought into unexpected relationship in landscapes or interiors. There remain some remarkable works of this period: 'La rencontre', 'La chambre du devin', 'L'homme du large', 'La naissance de l'idole', among many others. They all reveal in their composition a feeling for Chirico. This sympathy is evident even in the titles; for example, 'Le ménage de l'inventeur' or 'Le retour de l'explorateur'. At the same time works like 'Panorama populaire', 'L'aube á Cayenne', and particularly 'L'assassin menacé', indicated that the painter was capable of further developments.

Rightly or wrongly advised by friends, at the end of 1927 Magritte decided to leave the Brussels suburb where he had been living for many years and to settle, near Paris, at Nogent-le-Perreux on the River Marne. There he was in frequent touch with the poets André Breton and Paul Eluard, the Surrealist leaders.

Although Magritte was not very happy in France (he left three years later to return to Belgium) it was at Le Perreux that he produced a great variety of work in which he proved himself the master of his own intentions. All traces of the Chirico manner had vanished, and each picture became somehow a new invention, to which he applied the required execution and style.

The contribution of Chirico's genius, in his work from 1911 to 1917, was the creation of a *frisson* of fatality in each of his paintings, placing some secular 'mystery' before the onlooker. From 1928 Magritte went beyond Chirico; he pursued 'mystery' to its dialectical conclusion: the 'non-mystery', the poetic matter-of-fact.

Unlike most modern imaginative artists, who have used all sorts of simplified, hasty, or allusive techniques to further their expressive ends, Magritte depicts the elements in his paintings with a conventional realistic care. But it is obvious that this technique is not what matters to the painter essentially. He uses such a technique in order to give to each poetic element its full effect and to achieve the maximum contrast or inter-relation with the other elements in the composition.

Magritte's methods of representation are intimately linked with his major aim. It may be that these methods and this aim would be equally unpalatable to an Academician or to an Action painter.

If Picasso has influenced scores of artists and has been aped all over the world, it is not on account of his genius but simply because of his traditionalism and eclecticism. Magritte is inimitable, except by himself. Therefore there is little danger of witnessing a wave of 'Magrittism'. Magritte occupies in the arts today a position completely distinct from those painters who compete with each other within the favoured aesthetic trends of the moment.

Magritte's reputation now grows steadily. Every year his work occupies a larger place in important European and American collections. Recently his prestige has been considerably enhanced in Great Britain by the exhibitions of the J. B. Urvater Collection, at Leicester, York, Belfast, and the Tate Gallery, where ten works were shown. The long-term loan to the Tate of that important work, 'La durée poignardée', from the Edward James Collection, has also helped to remove from the younger generations of art critics the hostility to which their elders gave vent twenty years ago. Too often surrealist paintings were called 'literary'. It is still useful to underline the fact that poetic painting such as that of Magritte is not 'literary'. On the walls of museums and galleries in Great Britain and elsewhere there remain enough 'literary' (anecdotic, explanatory) paintings of the nineteenth century to enable anyone to make comparisons.

Simple and modest, René Magritte lives now in a medium-sized house in Brussels, pursuing his search for more 'poetic evidence' with which to enrich the imaginations of those who are able to enter and share his world.

'Au seuil de la liberté,' 1929
Coll. J. B. Urvater, Brussels

'Perspective' (Madame de Récamier), 1950
Private Collection, U.S.A.

'Les travaux d'Alexandre'
1955
Jolas Gallery, New York

'L'art de la conversation', 1948. *Coll. Peter de Marel, New York*

'La magie noire', I, 1934
Coll. *Mme Happé-Lorge, Brussels*

'Le thérapeute', II, 1937
Coll. J. B. Urvater, Brussels

'La révélation du présent', 1936. *Coll. Marc Hendrickx, Brussels*

'Le pont d'Héraclite', 1932. *Coll. Abel Giandolini, London*

'La reconnaissance infinie', 1932. *Coll. Claude Spaak, Paris*

'La durée poignardée,' 1939. *Coll. Edward James (at Tate Gallery, London)*

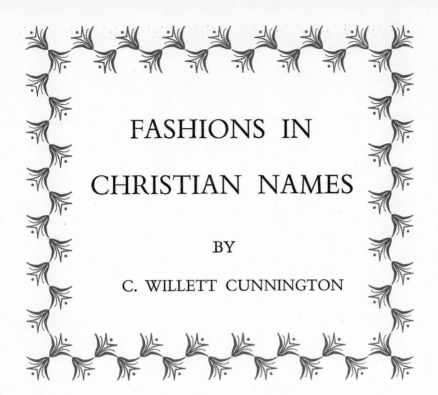

FASHIONS IN

CHRISTIAN NAMES

BY

C. WILLETT CUNNINGTON

CHRISTIAN names cost nothing. Even the poorest can give their children as many as they like. Here, then, is the cheapest of luxuries, to be indulged in, seemingly, without restrictions. In fact, however, popular taste has always been selective, and analysis of half a million examples in the last six centuries reveals that a 'repertoire' of some three hundred names for each sex has sufficed, worn-out names being replaced by new from time to time, with a stalwart band of old favourites apparently immortal.

A characteristic common to all periods has been the belief, more or less consciously felt, that the name chosen may in some way or other affect the child's future. It is the nature of this belief that has changed, step by step, from the spiritual to the mundane, marked by a procession of fashions.

The medieval preference was for the name of a Saint who would give the child special protection. The Reformation developed the notion of a more direct appeal to the Deity, and soon the name became a positive assertion of divine approval. The seventeenth century encouraged a fundamental breach with tradition by a fashion for names entirely devoid of religious significance, a mode expanding in the eighteenth century into those specifically suggestive of Class Distinction and Sex Appeal. Since then, as fresh sources of supplies have been discovered, a mass of ephemeral names have come and gone, few novelties having taken root.

One might have expected to find the name of a sovereign to be most commonly used during his reign, but this has not been the case. The belief that a king was semi-divine, whose name it would therefore be improper to borrow, may have been a restraint which, however, lapsed at his decease. Thus the christenings recorded during a reign throw light on the popularity or otherwise of the *preceding* monarch.

By this test King John, described by historians as one of the worst of our kings, must have been, in fact, most popular. When his reign began in A.D. 1199 the name John, though borne by two important Saints, was extremely rare. Thirty years after it had ended, a fourth of the boys of England had been given that name, and by 1400 30 per cent—in some places 50 per cent—of all males were called John. The resulting confusion, for taxing purposes, was such that surnames had to be invented.

All over the country the name remained first favourite, in spite of changes of dynasties and creeds, becoming, in 'John Bull', a national symbol. Today, in a list of some 1,500 schoolboys, John easily tops the rest, a compliment which would have tickled the humour of that disreputable sovereign.

Almost as unexpected has been the fortune of Elizabeth, a name abruptly becoming a favourite at the death in 1503 of the wife of Henry VII, the saintly Elizabeth of York, who died broken-hearted at the loss of her eldest son. Among girls' names it had sprung from fifth favourite (8 per cent) to first (13·4 per cent) even before Elizabeth I had come to the throne. During her reign it then reached 14 per cent—the only instance of a reigning sovereign's name being first favourite—but it did not reach its maximum of popularity until the Commonwealth (18·2 per cent). Unlike John's, however, Elizabeth's name was never popular everywhere; far less in the west than the east of the country, and always most in London. It was not a name likely to find favour among Catholics or extreme Puritans.

Records show that Henry has never been a popular name, George only in late Victorian times, and James not until the Stuarts had been forgotten. The name of the great Saxon king, Alfred, seems to have been

suppressed by the Normans, and it almost wholly disappeared for seven centuries until about 1800, when it was unearthed by antiquaries, to flourish during the nineteenth century, and then, once more, to become forgotten.

Of regal names, William has had a unique career. Without any saintly association, without the support of any heroic figure since the Conqueror or of any subsequent sovereign of note, William remained second favourite all over England throughout the Middle Ages, through dynasty after dynasty and century after century, until the nineteenth century, when it rose to first favourite. We do well to call its progenitor 'the Conqueror'; unaided he defied the Hagiology itself. What gave his name its magic? The fact that he alone had ever conquered us? Was it a symbol of superhuman power? How appropriate that in these unheroic days the name should now have shrunk to a shadow.

There have, of course, been causes more profound and insidious than the influence of an individual producing changes of popular taste in Christian names. Some of these deserve the historian's attention. We are taught, for instance, that the Reformation was the act of Henry VIII and its official date 1534. But it seems that the ground had been shifting for fifty years; the old attachment to Saints' names had been loosening; those of abstract virtues (Faith, Grace, Mercy, etc.), together with Biblical names that were not those of Saints (Adam, Reuben, Jeremiah), were creeping in, suggestive of a direct claim to divine approval. This was the basis of the Protestant idea and it was surely significant that within a few years of Luther's famous challenge of 1517 a boy was actually christened in a London church Luthomo (Luther-Homo, 'Luther is the man'). Meanwhile, names from pagan sources such as Hector, Hercules, and Lucretia were being fancied by the educated classes. All this before 1534.

In the course of the sixteenth century the Protestant impulse produced two distinct fashions of names; one merely indicated that the child had become 'christianized', and for this purpose any Biblical name served equally well. By the end of Elizabeth's reign one might have seen Delilah and Jezebel playing on the village green with their brothers Ananias and baby Methusalah.

As familiarity with the Scriptures spread among simple earnest folk, they were searched for rare and precious specimens. Before long a Nebuchadnezzar blossomed in Bedfordshire, a Holophernes in

Suffolk, and at least three Cornish boys answered—more or less—to Mahershalalhashbaz.

We have to distinguish such Protestant names from the Puritan, which claimed spiritual or moral excellence in such names as Innocent, Accepted, or Faithful, a claim becoming increasingly confident as the Puritans became more powerful; their boys then staggered under the distinction of being Righteous, Much-Mercie, or Fromabove, a couple of brothers being Preserved and More-Fruit. Their girls might be Triumphe, Perform-Thy-Vows, Paradise, or merely Godlie.

Equally characteristic was the Puritan taste for names suggestive of exceptional sinners, their children grovelling under such names as Humiliation, Admonition, or Repentance. We find an Essex married couple, the man named Affliction and his wife Adose. Illegitimates were branded with Baseborn, Renote Magdalen, Fly-Fornication, and the like, but research has failed to discover those fantastical chain-names reading like texts, much ridiculed by later writers but which appear to have existed, if at all, as a sort of *nom de guerre* assumed by Roundhead soldiers.

Nor were the assertive Puritan names ever common or widely distributed, being practically unknown in the northern half of the kingdom. In such regions as those where Puritanism was rife we find curious signs of attempts to ridicule those boastful claims; names such as Godsgift or Safe-on-High might be burlesqued as Freegift and Uncertaine, and a bucolic humour chose names that composed puns with the surnames; for example, the surnames being in brackets: Called (Lower), Fromabove (Downe), Just (Wass), Plumb (Innocent), Luke (Sharpe), Jolly (Sadd), Prim (Rose).

The desire for social distinction led in the seventeenth century to the introduction of multiple names. James I was our first sovereign to have more than one. The fashion rapidly spread among the Upper Classes; it was found advantageous for a débutante to be adorned with 'jewels five words long'. Horace Walpole tells of a foxhunting squire whose daughter, endowed with the names Louisa Maria Sobieski Foxhunter Moll Boycott, married an earl.

The seventeenth century also developed the use of surnames as Christian names, by which means one could suggest relationship with aristocratic families. As a result, a great many surnames became permanently converted (e.g. Stanley, Howard, Neville, Montague), and today about a third of the male Christian names in use derive from surnames.

[288]

There was nothing to prevent such fashions from being copied by the common people. A Suffolk village couple in 1791 called their daughter Louisa Valentine Danvers Augusta Frederica; but such folk were usually content with a blunderbuss loaded with bits of several names; such as Mickipheralphry, Christopheranna, Iliamgarath, or Stonemma, indicating that the child had two parents. But what simpler proof than the name concocted by the Gloucestershire couple who called their boy Bothenet?

The search for unusual names led the more educated to explore pagan sources. As soon as Ariosto's romance was translated in 1591, a Shrewsbury gentleman proudly named his son Orlando Furioso. In the seventeenth century Pythagoras, Endymion, Narcissus, Venus, and Parthenia had become acceptable Christian names. An eighteenth-century country parson was sufficiently broad-minded to christen his son Bacchus.

The Christian name can also exert a subtle degree of sex appeal. Among girls' names, those having a 'feminine ending'—that is, an unaccentuated last syllable, as in Dorothy, Margery, Cicely—are given by it a soft 'womanly' quality of sound. It is significant that such girls' names were fewer in the Elizabethan half-century than ever before or since. No Shakespearian heroine has such a type of name; incidentally, *Love's Labour's Lost* (1590) has only seven lines with feminine endings, whereas *Cymbeline* (1610) has over seven hundred. Presumably the Elizabethans did not like weak verse or 'womanly' young women. The young men liked them to be tough and to sound it, e.g. Catren, Gartright, Joan, Maudlen, Emmot, Bennet. In the seventeenth and eighteenth centuries, however, the proportion of names with feminine endings increased rapidly, until 25 per cent of girls possessed them. We find Pally, Mally, Lovey, Cherry, Betty, or, more alluring still, Joyous, Honeysuckle, Nice, Darling, Pleasant, Freelove.

The Victorians shrank from so outspoken an appeal and preferred nice girls to resemble botanical specimens. Primroses, Violets, Lilys, Rosies, and Buttercups bloomed hopefully; described by a woman writer in 1889 as 'Sweet girls! How like the living flowers they are! What a sense of sunshine and purity they bring with them!' Today, floral attributes are in less demand.

By the eighteenth century the Christian name had obviously acquired a new importance, especially for girls; it should imply, if not blue blood, then at least warm. The search for names charged with feeling was helped by the spread of new novels from the circulating library.

Though denounced by Sir Anthony Absolute as 'an evergreen tree of diabolical knowledge' the novel supplied the latest fashion in heroines' names. Fielding's *Joseph Andrews* (1742) popularized the name Fanny, and in 1794 the first English thriller, *The Mysteries of Udolpho*, established Emily as a name of irresistible charm. Oceans of tears were shed over Emily's vicissitudes. Catherine Morland devoured *The Mysteries of Udolpho* in two days, 'my hair standing on end the whole time'. Alas, its decline in public favour carried with it the name of its heroine.

Fiction has played odd tricks with Christian names, and none stranger than with Alice. In the fifteenth century some 12 per cent of girls bore that name, but after the Reformation its appeal steadily declined until in the first half of the nineteenth century it had almost vanished. Then, in 1865, *Alice in Wonderland* appeared. Immediately the name was hailed as an ideal symbol of innocent girlhood, an epitome of maidenly purity. It bounded into favour, to become, for the rest of that century, the most popular girls' name of any. Now the name no longer thrills; searching a current list of 1,600 schoolgirls I murmur, 'Alice, where art thou?', but there is no answer—no, not one.

A plethora of fame can be disastrous to a name; after *Jane Eyre* had appeared in 1847 that name was considered in refined circles to be scarcely ladylike; Jane slumped from 5 per cent of girls' names to 1·2 per cent and was relegated to the servants' hall, a synonym for a housemaid. Mabel, once a medieval name of repute, succumbed to a comic song; and *Little Lord Fauntleroy* produced such a surfeit of Cedrics that the public stomach has not yet recovered.

Have you noticed the absence of certain once-popular names? That there are few Algernons or Marmadukes or Ethels about? Such negative fashions can be very informative. In the Middle Ages, for instance, there was a notable rarity of the name Mary, thought too sacred for sinful mortals to borrow. The Reformation abolished this taboo; the name became rapidly popular, and topped the list by 1700, when one in five girls were so-called. Its original association becoming forgotten, it served the Victorians as a convenient name for a cook.

Throughout the Middle Ages the name Peter was shunned for an opposite reason, its association with the hateful tax of 'Peter's Pence'. Later it was thought to savour of Popery. It did not become popular until the present century.

The exploits of Titus Oates rendered that hitherto respectable Biblical

name unclean and henceforth fit only for villains in melodrama. If you want a more recent example of a taboo there is the once-admired aristocratic name of Adolphus. What mother today would call her son Adolf?

While popular taste is readily affected by any widespread wave of emotion the English character seems to present a stubborn resistance to official propaganda. When Edward III announced in 1349 that henceforth St George of Cappadocia was to be the national Saint the mass of the people would have nothing to do with that foreign import. They possessed, already, a perfectly satisfactory native Saint of their own, St Thomas of Canterbury, whose tomb they could visit and of whose miraculous powers they had abundant evidence. The name George remained, therefore, an obscure rarity, while Thomas rose from 6 per cent of males in the thirteenth century to nearly 15 per cent by 1500. Henry VIII's attempts to denigrate the Canterbury Saint did not affect in the slightest the popularity of Thomas, which remained in the first three favourite boys' names until Victorian times.

After the battle of Bosworth and the accession of Henry VII, official Tudor propaganda sought to blacken the character of Richard III. The popularity of that name, however, remained unshaken until the middle of the eighteenth century, when Garrick's playing of the name part in Shakespeare's melodrama and the horrid association of Richard with the 'wicked uncle' caused the name almost to vanish for nearly a century.

It is evident that a Christian name possesses, to a variable degree, an emotional tone derived primarily from its original association; but subsequent events may completely change the nature of this emotional tone, turning an agreeable name into a disagreeable. More commonly, however, the emotional tone becomes just worn away by long usage and is replaced by a mildly pleasant sense of familiarity. Just look at the Christian names that are most popular today: the boys' list is headed by John, David, and Michael; the girls' by Margaret and Ann. All of them Saints, you see, but without their haloes.

Victorian song-title: 'Married to a Mermaid', sung by Mr Arthur Lloyd

THE NATURAL HISTORY
OF THE MERMAID

by Richard Carrington

THE MERMAID is perhaps the most glamorous and poetic figure in the whole history of mythology and folklore. To study her natural history may therefore seem a little unchivalrous, and I do not propose to treat it with the scientific precision appropriate to, say, jellyfish or hake. My method will be simply to trace some of the influences, natural, psychological, and spiritual, that have given the mermaid her unique place in the imaginations of men.

First, let us see how she has manifested herself on various occasions to human eyes. Working backwards from our own times, we find that there has been a distressing lack of mermaid sightings during the whole of the present century. This can possibly be put down to the increasing gravity of scientists, who have become dispirited under the vast accumulations of facts that press each year more heavily upon their minds; it may also be due to the amenities of modern ports, which have largely distracted mariners from their traditional occupation of conjuring glamorous visions from the depths of the sea. But in the nineteenth century a less prosaic spirit was abroad, as is shown by the following letter written to *The Times* in 1809 by a Mr William Munro, a schoolmaster of Thurso in Scotland. It was headed, 'The Mermaid Seen on the Coast of Caithness'.

Dear Sir—About twelve years ago, when I was a Parochial Schoolmaster at Reay, in the course of my walking on the shore of Sandside Bay, being a warm fine day in summer, I was induced to extend my walk towards Sandside Head, when my attention was arrested by the appearance of a figure resembling an unclothed human female, sitting upon a rock extending into the sea. . . . The forehead was round, the face plump, the cheeks ruddy, the eyes blue, the mouth and lips of a natural form . . . the breasts and abdomen, the arms and fingers of the size of a full grown body of the human species. It remained on the rock three or four minutes after I observed it, and was exercised during that period in combing its hair, which was long and thick, and of which it appeared proud, and then dropped into the sea, from which it did not reappear to me.

(Signed) WM. MUNRO

This was one of many nineteenth-century mermaid reports, some of which aroused widespread interest right up to the end of Queen Victoria's reign. The imaginations of our grandparents were, in fact, particularly mermaid-prone, for the concept of these mysterious maidens of the sea was in tune with the exaggerated romanticism of the time. Prints of mermaids were acceptable on the walls of even the staidest Victorian homes—probably because the presence of scales below the waist conveniently camouflaged any suggestion of the more basic attributes of sex. Such artists as Arnold Böcklin amassed vast fortunes with portraits of wild-eyed sirens tossed among the waves of tempestuous seas, while even such respectable poets as Tennyson occasionally indulged in images of

> Sweet faces, rounded arms, and bosoms prest
> To little harps of gold.

On a somewhat lower plane, sentimental siren songs, such as Arthur Lloyd's 'Married to a Mermaid', were a feature of every music hall in the 'eighties.

Pressing back farther into time, physical observations of alleged mermaids become increasingly common. The eighteenth century, usually thought of as an age of scepticism and good sense, produced a particularly good crop. Several eighteenth-century mermaids apparently lived off British coasts, while others were seen in regions as far apart as the Arctic and the East Indies.

A Dutch colonial chaplain named François Valentijn reproduced in his *Natural History of Amboina* (1726) a delightful picture of an East Indian mermaid with other queer fish of the region. From the caption we learn that the mermaid was fifty-nine inches long, lived after being caught for four days and seven hours in a barrel filled with water, and 'uttered little cries like those of a mouse'. In spite of these vocal limitations, its figure, at least the upper part, had such obvious attractions that King George III was graciously pleased to accept the original picture, and Peter the Great of Russia wrote to Valentijn for further details. These unfortunately the Dutchman was unable to provide, but he intrigued the Czar with an account of another episode in which a mermaid and a merman were seen swimming together by more than fifty persons. 'Should the stubborn world hesitate to believe it,' he adds, 'it matters nothing, for

[294]

there are people who would deny the existence of Rome, Constantinople, or Cairo, simply because they themselves have not happened to see them.'

Although the testimony of schoolmasters and chaplains is obviously of the highest value, an even more impressive account comes from the rugged old seventeenth-century navigator Henry Hudson. The incident occurred off Nova Zembla during one of Hudson's daring attempts to force the North-West Passage, and he describes his mermaid with the same sang-froid as you and I might report the sighting of a porpoise:

This evening [June 15] one of our company, looking overboard, saw a mermaid, and, calling up some of the company to see her, one more of the crew came up, and by that time she was come close to the ship's side, looking earnestly on the men. A little after a sea came and overturned her. From the navel upward, her back and breasts were like a woman's, as they say that saw her; her body as big as one of us, her skin very white, and long hair hanging down behind, of colour black. In her going down they saw her tail, which was like the tail of a porpoise, speckled like a mackerel.

References to mermaids occur in medieval and Renaissance natural histories and collections of travellers' tales, but these almost always

Arnold Böcklin: 'Der Meeremadchen'

seem to be based on hearsay rather than direct observation. Most of them can safely be regarded as springing from a fevered imagination, an elaborate flight of alcoholic fantasy, misinterpretation of inadequate facts, and in some cases straightforward honest-to-God lying. To take an example, there is the tale of seven mermen and mermaids captured at Manaar in 1560, and carried to Goa, where they were dissected by Demas Bosquez, physician to the Viceroy, and 'their internal structure found to be in all respects conformable to the human'. Another account speaks of a merman seen off the coast of Martinique which was approached so closely by several persons that it was seen to wipe its hands across its face and even heard to blow its nose.

Setting such pleasing concepts aside, is it possible to trace any logical pattern in the mermaid legend and to account for its wide distribution and long persistence in human tradition? To answer this question we must turn first to the evolution of primitive religion and the history of classical myth and legend, and second to the accounts given by modern science of animals of mermaid-like form.

Our primitive ancestors, we now know, did not recognize one god, as do the majority of western religions today, but worshipped a number of different objects, persons, and natural forces, each in a different form. Thus there was a separate god for the sun, the moon, and the stars; gods for the rivers, mountains, and lakes; and gods associated with man-made objects such as household goods, weapons, and even agricultural implements. The most important gods were those associated with the more powerful and dramatic natural forces. Hence the great power ascribed by our ancestors to the sun-god, who supplied light and warmth to the world, and to the rain-god, who brought fertility to the parched earth after drought.

One of the most awe-inspiring natural phenomena, to our ancestors as to ourselves, was the sea, and numerous gods and goddesses were associated with it at different times in different regions. Some of these deities were likewise associated with the legend of the Flood—a legend which occurs not only in the Old Testament, but in modified form in many ancient religions and even in the mythologies of primitive peoples today. It is among these water deities of the sea and the Flood that we must seek for the origin of the mermaid legend.

The progenitor of all the glamorous mermaids of later times was in all probability not a woman but a man; yet not quite a man, but a

fish deity who came up from the Persian Gulf and landed on the shores of Babylonia to teach the inhabitants of that land the values of civilization. The authority for this story is a priest and astronomer of Babylon known as Berosus, who recorded it in his *History of Syria*, written about 260 B.C. The fish-god was mainly worshipped at Erech, 'the place of the ark', where he was known as Oannes. Elsewhere he was known variously as Oes, Hoa, Ea, Ana, Aun, and Oan, and was also sometimes identified with the Biblical Noah himself. He was usually represented as a typical merman, with the bearded head and torso of a man, and a scaly tail below the waist. But some pictures show him as a normal man with a fish's head worn as a cap, the skin hanging down his back in the form of a cloak. Another Babylonian god, Dagon, is likewise sometimes represented in this double form. Scholars still remain cautious about regarding Dagon as a sea-god, but the poet Milton had no such reservations:

> Dagon his name; sea monster, upward man
> And downward fish.

The earliest female ancestor of the mermaid in human belief is probably the Semitic moon-goddess Atergatis, or Derceto. Lucian described her as having 'the half of a woman, and from the thighs downwards a fish's tail'. We may be surprised that a moon-goddess should have had such a decidedly fishy shape, but there is an interesting reason for this. Our ancestors observed that the moon often rose from the sea, and returned to it once more when its course over the night sky was run. It was clear that during the hours when the moon-goddess was invisible beneath the ocean she must be endowed with the power of swimming. That her shape should be partially fish-like was therefore reasonable enough.

Apart from such important deities as Oannes, Dagon, and Atergatis, the sea spawned a great host of other mermaid ancestors and relations. Typical of these were the tritons, who were not, as is generally believed, exclusively male, but included true mermaids who acted as attendants to sea divinities. Incidentally, the tritons also produced a remarkable subspecies in the creatures known as ichthyocentaurs, or centauro-tritons. These had the forefeet of a horse as well as human upper parts and a fish's tail.

Another group of mythological figures ancestral to the mermaids

were the sirens. These were the offspring of the river-god Achelous and one of those attractive nymphs who seem to have been so readily available to the more influential gods in Greek mythology. They were represented in earlier art by birds with the heads of women, and later by women with the legs of birds. They are never correctly shown with a fish-like tail, this not having been one of their aids to allure, but they greatly influenced the mermaid legend by their character. The sirens were regarded as the very acme of marine sex appeal, luring mariners to destruction by their seductive movements and beguiling songs quite as effectively as the modern bikini girl ensnares incautious millionaires with a sinuous walk and a repertoire of husky contralto compliments. The treacherous beauty of the sirens was later transferred to the true mermaids, who were alleged to be irresistible to any male lucky enough to observe one.

As classical science evolved, doubts began to arise as to whether tritons, sirens, and mermaids were real or imaginary creatures. Myth and legend played such an important part in classical life that they often became confused with reality, and to the ordinary person the existence of mermaids would have been as indisputable as the existence of cod. But following on the more scientific approach to natural history which originated with the work of Aristotle a greater degree of scepticism began to prevail. Learned men demanded a more palpable proof of the existence and nature of living things than could be provided by oral tradition and unsupported travellers' tales. Nevertheless, the magical element in natural science persisted, and even Pliny, the matter-of-fact cavalry officer who wrote the second great work of natural science in the history of the world, defended the existence of mermaids with a gallantry worthy of his profession and rank. In the words of his seventeenth-century English translator, Philemon Holland, he writes: 'And as far as the Meremaids, it is no fabulous tale that goeth of them: for looke how painters draw them, so they are indeed: only their bodie is rough and skaled all over, even in those parts where they resemble a woman. For such a Meremaid was seene and beheld plainely upon a coast neere to the shore: and the inhabitants dwelling neer, heard it a farre off when it was a dying, to make pitteous mone, crying and chattering very heavily.'

The belief that mermaids were real creatures persisted, as we have seen, throughout the Middle Ages and Renaissance, and in some quarters into the period of living memory. In the nineteenth century it was reinforced by the appearance in Europe and America of a number of stuffed mermaids which were put on exhibition by enterprising showmen. These, it was claimed, had been caught in eastern waters by intrepid fishermen, and must be regarded as final and unquestionable proof of the mermaid's real existence. Many, indeed, accepted the stuffed mermaids as the last word on the subject, and quite rejected the statements of experts who said that these creatures were concocted from the rear of a fish and the upper part of a monkey cleverly sewn together at the waist.

Now what has modern science to say concerning the mermaid legend? Zoologists of the best sort are not usually of an unromantic disposition, but the disciplines of their science cannot unfortunately be stretched quite far enough to admit the existence of real mermaids. It is obvious, they say, that the numerous observations made during the history of the legend must be based on cases of mistaken identity. If this is so, what animals of the sea are most likely to have caused the error?

Two groups of animals are usually favoured for this romantic role: the seals of the family *Phocidae* and the order of *Sirenia* or sirens, known to the less poetic naturalists as sea-cows. It is certainly possible that seals have been responsible for many of the mermaid reports originating in northern and temperate waters, including the glamorous vision vouchsafed to Mr William Munro off the coast of Caithness. Those who have only observed seals as captives in the zoo will have little idea how mermaid-like they can look when seen from a cliff-top in the wild. Their bodies taper to a point, resembling the typical mermaid tail, their hand-like fore-flippers have a most human character, and their plump, expressive faces and soft intelligent eyes are considerably more attractive than those of most of the human females available to mariners in British ports. Moreover, they have a habit of lying in languid attitudes on rocks, or poising themselves in the water when swimming so that only the fore-part of their bodies protrudes above the surface. Many naturalists have commented on their human appearance when in such poses, and it is easy to see how a glimpse of a seal at dusk or in a stormy sea could lead an untrained observer to suppose he had seen a mermaid.

The mermaid sightings in tropical waters are more likely to have been accounted for by a member of the order of sea-cows. This name (admittedly a most unfortunate one in the present context) is borne by only three familiar species, two living and one extinct. The extinct species, known as *Rhytina stelleri*, or Steller's sea-cow, was killed off only a little over a hundred years ago, and could thus have played a part in the mermaid legend. But as it grew regularly to between twenty and thirty feet long, and few observers have described mermaids quite as robust as this, the honour is better left to the two smaller living sea-cows, known respectively as the manatee and the dugong.

Both these creatures inhabit tropic coasts. The manatee lives in the rivers and estuaries of eastern America and western Africa; the dugong in the Indian Ocean and along the shores of Australia and the East Indies. The resemblance of these animals to mermaids is based on their general anatomical shape rather than any special pretensions to glamour. Their bodies are about the same size as a woman's, they have hand-like fore-limbs, and their ample, rounded breasts are in the human position on the upper part of the trunk. There are no hind limbs at all, and the body tapers to a horizontally flattened tail. In other respects they have few charms except great mildness of temperament. They have a thick, cleft upper lip, and a somewhat vacant expression; the dugong's face is decidedly whiskered. Yet these characteristics are only apparent to close inspection, and it is by no means unlikely that some of the mermaid reports from Africa and Asia have been inspired by a distant or indistinct view of a sea-cow in the act of submerging.

There we can say that the natural history of the mermaid is at an end. In spite of the belated intrusion of seals and sea-cows into the picture the story is not without romance. It began in the questing spirits of our ancestors, who conjured from the chaos of the waters a vision of a god symbolizing the majesty of the sea and the wonder that lies at the heart of the natural world. From these cosmic beginnings the hunger for glamour in the souls of men produced a vision at once more human and more alluring, more sensual and more dangerous—a vision of beauty in the form of a woman with a fish's tail. This infinitely desirable being manifested herself in many guises according to the age and region in which she was conceived—as Atergatis, the goddess of the moon, as the sirens, beckoning Ulysses and his heroic companions to destruction on a rocky island of the western sea, and as the mermaid herself, a haunting and mysterious symbol of human desire. If at last we find that the familiar seal and the stolid sea-cow have played a part in creating this symbol we need not be unduly depressed, for these animals too are part of the universal wonder in the world. They share with the mermaid a secure place in man's impassioned vision of the universe around him.

Early nineteenth-century engraving, artist unknown

MY CONTRIBUTION
TO ANGLO-AMERICAN FRIENDSHIP

BY FRED BASON

ONE OF THE nicest surprises of my life was when I was made an honorary member of the Mark Twain Society of America. The president of the Society is Harry Truman. The only other two honorary members in Europe are Sir Winston Churchill and John Masefield. So I'm in good company. This honour—and a lovely engraved scroll to prove it—came to me, said the Secretary, because of my efforts towards international goodwill.

You'll be asking what I've done to deserve this. Well, until I was fifteen I'd never had a new suit or overcoat. Everything I wore was second-hand —cast-off clothing bought by my mother off barrows in the streets. Not that she was *all* that poor; but I had come late into the world, when my father and mother were over forty, and I wasn't really wanted. Because I was lonely I looked for friends. I found a lot of them in books: that's why I became a bookseller. I found a lot more by asking for their autographs. (On January 3rd, 1959, I obtained my twelve-thousandth autograph: it was Lenny the Lion and Terry Hall—a favourite TV act of mine. Having been a Big Name Hunter all my life I thought I'd be a Big Game Hunter for once, and off I went to Birmingham to collect the autograph of a lion.)

I've not only collected 12,000 autographs, but I've got some 15,000 addresses of folks who have been friendly to me in the passing years. I store them in boot and shoe boxes. In the winter I take down one of these boxes and spend a whole day writing to people overseas from whom I haven't heard in years.

Last December I happened to pick up a goodbye letter I had had from Aileen Stanley when she returned to America over thirty years ago. 'Who's Aileen?' some of you may ask. 'And what's she got to do with you?' Turn back, regular readers, to page 147 in *The Saturday Book*, No. 11, and you will read how, when I was fifteen, I landed myself a part-time job as head cook and bottle-getter to a Vaudeville Star. Well, that Vaudeville Star was Aileen Stanley. *Now* you remember her! She was a top-liner—original singer of 'Over on the Sunny Side' and 'Souvenirs'. From the time I was fifteen until I was eighteen I adored her. I would have died for her. She bought me my first new suit and my first new overcoat. And it was her kindness to me that pioneered my contribution to Anglo-American friendship.

When I picked up her farewell letter again I thought I'd let her know that now I'm famous (the world's most famous genuine Cockney author, that's me) I can get a new overcoat *free*.

How's this? you ask. Some years ago I invented a slogan for a firm in Birmingham — 'Swallow Raincoats never get the Bird'. (In case any of you far-flung readers don't know what 'the Bird' is, it's a Cockney term of disapproval, called elsewhere 'the Raspberry'.) Well, I exchanged that slogan for a free raincoat. Each year the Swallow people send me a thousand postcards printed with a nice photograph of myself wearing my raincoat, and with these postcards I make my contribution to international goodwill.

Coming back to Aileen, I picked up one of these Swallow postcards and wrote her a line on it, reminding her that she bought me my very first overcoat. Thirty-two years it is since I saw her, but back comes a letter from her—a lovely, sweet, tender letter that makes life worth living.

The world ain't so bad; and some of the nicest people in it are the most famous. Take Mary Pickford, for instance. Thirty years ago I was broke to the wide. I looked and felt a street-urchin: the knees were out of my trousers. Although she'd said she was not granting interviews to the Press Mary Pickford talked to me for five minutes—mostly about religion, and she meant every word—and the five guineas I earned from that interview put me on my feet again.

There was an actress! I don't suppose she remembers, but it was exactly fifty years ago that she made her first picture. Her mother took her along to D. W. Griffith, who gave her a part in a film called *Her First Biscuits*. It was completed in one day, April 20th, 1909; its length was 481 feet, and it ran for six minutes.

All Mary Pickford did in it was to try and eat a very hard biscuit.

Mary Pickford has given delight to millions in the past fifty years, but to nobody more than me. In 1941, when my home was blitzed, her autograph went up in dust. I sat down and wrote to her, asking if she'd replace it. I addressed the letter 'Mary Pickford, United States of America'. Soon came a letter in her own hand saying, 'How very kind of you to ask *me* for my autograph.' And a little while later came a food parcel, 'in case I was hungry'. I shared that parcel with ten other folks, and all of us blessed a very sweet lady.

The Americans—I love 'em. Many's the invitation I've had to go and stay with them, but somehow it's never happened. On December 19th, 1938, I had a card from Helen Morgan, then a celebrated cabaret star, and one of the original cast of *Show Boat*. She wrote: 'Come and see me. All expenses paid. Ring 2194 Hudson, N.Y.C. on arrival. Helen Morgan.' If I'd taken the ship I planned to take I should have arrived on the day of her funeral.

However, here at 152 Westmoreland Road, S.E.17 (ten minutes from Big Ben, fifteen minutes from Bow Bells) I've given hospitality to something like five hundred Americans since the war. They knock at my door. Then: 'Say, Buddy, I read Vol. 12 of the *Saturday Book* way out in Chicago, and I said to myself if I ever reach old London I will call on that fellow Bason—and here I am!' Lizzie, my landlady, (yes, she's well, thank you) immediately gets the visitor a meal or whisky or tea (the whisky comes from

Mr. W. James of Willenhall—a loyal *Saturday Book* reader—my own slender means would not run to 37s. 6d. a bottle!), I stop whatever work I am engaged upon, and, if the American visitor is new to London, I make myself tidy, put on my Swallow raincoat, and take him out for an hour or two and show him all the odd and unusual parts of London that he won't find in a Guide Book.

Last night I had an American visitor, a parson, about twenty-eight. He had been hitch-hiking all over Europe. He stood at the door and said: 'J. Denton Anderson told me to look you up if I ever reached London.' It was a bitter cold night. Lizzie made him hot coffee. He stayed nearly two hours talking philosophy and religion. I asked where he was bound for when he left us. 'Oh,' he said, 'I'm going to Leeds.' I said it was rather late to get a train to Leeds. 'Train,' he said. 'I don't use trains! I'll hitch-hike there, to a vicar I know just outside Leeds. I shall easily get a lift—it isn't far.' I wanted to give him hospitality for the night. He wouldn't hear of it.

Strange people—lovable people— these Americans. He looked a very ordinary man, but he was a very extraordinary man. This was not the first American visitor to my home who has hitch-hiked all over Europe. I remember a school teacher named Marty Bucco who did the same thing. He was no more than twenty. What astounded me was the fact that he had been all over Europe and *still did not possess an overcoat*! I asked whatever did he do when it rained or snowed, and he said so matter-of-factly: 'Stand under cover. I travel light.' And he did. All he had for four months in Europe was in a small haversack, and it didn't weigh six pounds.

So you see the sort of thing I do as my little contribution to Anglo-American friendship. It isn't much, but I get a kick out of it. Not so long ago I got a photograph from an American lady, on the back of which was written (yes, it's genuine: the Editor's seen it!): 'Dear Fred, I have heard that you are a lonesome bachelor and that you like books and collect autographs. Then surely you and I should get along just perfect. For I have Gibbon's *Decline and Fall* (unabridged) tattooed on my back, Tolstoy's *War and Peace* on my front—and Noël Coward has autographed me in an interesting spot. Yours for good reading, Lydia.' The photograph shows—from head to bust—a fully tattooed lady. As I say when I talk to Women's Guilds: 'Ladies, I'm single. I go to bed to *sleep*.' Wait for the laugh. Then: 'Well, I know of men who go to bed to *read*.'